M000223654

LIFE OF
NOBODY

REPARATION TO AFRICA:
"THE LAW OF KARMA IS STRONG"

EWA UNOKE Ph.D.

LIFE OF NOBODY
Copyright © 2021 by Ewa Unoke Ph.D.

All rights reserved. No part of this publication may be reproduced, distributed, or transmitted in any form or by any means, including photocopying, recording, or other electronic or mechanical methods, without the prior written permission of the publisher or author, except in the case of brief quotations embodied in critical reviews and certain other noncommercial uses permitted by copyright law.

Although every precaution has been taken to verify the accuracy of the information contained herein, the author and publisher assume no responsibility for any errors or omissions. No liability is assumed for damages that may result from the use of information contained within.

Library of Congress Control Number: 2021906282
ISBN-13: Hardback: 978-1-64749-424-7
Epub: 978-1-64749-425-4

Printed in the United States of America

 GoTo Publish

GoToPublish LLC
1-888-337-1724
www.gotopublish.com
info@gotopublish.com

CONTENTS

HOHA

Unvarnished Truthtelling

Olauda's story is more than a narrative about bondage and reparation, though slavery was a traumatic part of his life. It is the story of one Igbo teenager who encountered this brutal world and learned how to survive. In telling the story of one who survived, Olauda Ikwueno (my homie) tells the stories of countless others who did not. What is reparation for the long-muted voices we are not hearing?

PREFACE

How an enslaved and long-traumatized people should deal with the injustices of the past is a difficult one. In reckoning with the unhealed past, all the chapters in this book share a common theme – the danger of America and Europe ignoring the human rights abuses during and after slavery.

During the 1700s, the law allowed any European or American to own an African like a domestic animal. American and European slave-owners could force their African slaves to do whatever they wanted. Millions of such enslaved Igbo people (my relatives) had no human rights. My Igbo kinsmen and women worked under very hostile conditions and were bought and sold like cows and goats. Ezza (Igbo) ethnic people believe that the slave dealers' lands had been cursed, especially, Africa, America and Europe.

From slavery to freedom, the *difficulty of imagining* the African life persists until today. The life of the African woman or man outside the continent of Africa is the *Life of Nobody* - from Olauda Ikwueno, Malcolm X, Martin Luther King Jr to Breonna Taylor and George Floyd.

The loss of *power* and d*ignity* during the slave era has perpetually placed the Bantu-Negroid African in a different category... *others who are different.* Our African American relatives in the United States call this black problem - racism. Igbo Kamenuists – karma consciousness, free-thinkers and seekers of deeper truth, disagree. The *American Question* is not racism. It is an un-expiated national karma. After over two centuries, neither Africa nor America has succeeded in developing a *national mind* necessary to cohere into a redemptive *utsomini* (cleansing flood or deluge) for co-existence. Olauda is the symbol of Igbo people's long-struggle for justice and freedom – the **recognition** of the *Republic of Biafra*.

EWA UNOKE
KANSAS CITY, KANSAS, USA.
March 16, 2021

REDEMPTION SONG
Bob Marley

Old pirates, yes, they rob I
Sold I to the merchant ships
Minutes after they took I
From the bottomless pit
But my hand was made strong
By the hand of the almighty
We forward in this generation
Triumphantly
Won't you help to sing
These songs of freedom
'Cause all I ever have
Redemption songs
Redemption songs
Emancipate yourselves from mental slavery
None but ourselves can free our minds
Have no fear for atomic energy
'Cause none of them can stop the time
How long shall they kill our prophets
While we stand aside and look
Oh! Some say it's just a part of it
We've got to fulfill the book
Won't you help to sing
These songs of freedom
'Cause all I ever have
Redemption songs
Redemption songs
Redemption songs
Emancipate yourselves from mental slavery
None but ourselves can...

Source: Musixmatch

1

OLAUDA AS SYMBOL

Nduka: Life is the most precious
(Kamenuic Verses run through all the chapters, powerfully
unlocking the ethical teachings of the Ezza–Igbo people).

Portrait of Olauda from his book.

One day, in 1745, when the adults had left home to work in their farms, the unthinkable happened. Three Aro slave traders kidnapped Olauda Ikwueno, an eleven-year-old Igbo prince along with his sister. Both would never see their parents or home again. Olauda would soon be separated from his sister as well.

The enslaved Igbo prince would spend 10 years in West Indies, America, and Britain before he bought back his freedom in 1766.

In dealing with the unhealed past, what is the right thing to do? What is justice for Olauda and his sister? Pardon, prosecution, punishment or reparation? Would it make any difference to know that Olauda himself revealed that his father owned many slaves and somehow attributed his kidnapping with his sister to a Karmic consequence of his father's actions? Kamenuists (seekers of divine truth and virtuous living) would agree that Karma caught up with them. Their father 'reaped what he sowed.'

Kidnapped by his own people and sold to European trans-Atlantic slave traders, the Igbo prince Olauda Ikwueno, wrongly spelled "Olaudah Equiano" (my relative and kinsman) becomes a child of nobody and the bastard son of humanity. In captivity, without his Igbo faith and nation, he is like a warrior without his *nkogo* – sword. Without his Igbo faith, he will neither find spiritual truth nor physical freedom.

Consequently, when we discuss the critical issue of reparation, there are three central themes involved, namely, slavery, compensation, and the restoration of spiritual integrity. Olauda, in his own *Narrative* struggled for his spiritual and cultural identities. Without prejudice to the Euro-American concept of reparation, it is important to understand Olauda's indigenous faith - Kamenu which encourages adherents to "seek ye first the spiritual kingdom and everything else shall be added."

Therefore, when we ask white people to pay us for the historical wrongdoings of their ancestors, we have to make sure we are not creating new zones of Karma against white Americans instead of dissolving our past and present collective Karma.

Put differently, can you volunteer to be arrested, jailed or even hanged for the criminal acts of your parents or ancestors? Understanding the *law of karma* is crucial in our sacred quest for healing, reconciliation, and national recovery.

Believe it or not, Ezza Kamenuists warn us that Karma or the law of cause-and-effect is real. Any society which ignores this natural law does so at its own risk.

We are challenged by the most serious moral dilemma of our time. For too long, there have been intense debates on financial reparation to African Americans. Compensation to African American people, though well-meaning in intent, is essentially an economic remedy that ignores the African spiritual viewpoint. While the African slave narrative claims that most of the victims of the trans-Atlantic slave trade came from my Igbo ethnic nation, the Igbo people have been completely excluded from the reparation debate. However, despite the profundity of literature and debates so far, all have failed to examine the reparation discourses from the *Law of Karma* perspective. My argument here is that West African people especially Ndigbo (Igbo ethnic people also known as Biafrans) are morally and legally entitled to reparation after apologizing and atoning for their own human rights abuses during the trans-Atlantic slave trade.

But Nat Horowitz, my interlocutor in this discourse views the idea of Igbo reparation as a non-starter. "Compensation for Igbos including Aros? Excluding Aros? Compensation for all Africans, whether their ancestors or relatives were involved or not?"

2

AROCHUKWU

Ijenu: In the journey of life, some people are crying while others are rejoicing.
Arochukwu people (Aro), are the most controversial sub-ethnic group in Igboland.

The Aro dominated commerce, politics, and religion in precolonial times. During the trans-Atlantic slave trade in the fifteenth century, Aro people emerged as the notorious *underground conductors* and perpetrators of slavery in Igboland. The Aro's role in both precolonial and colonial times has shaped the way they are perceived in contemporary Igbo society.

The negative and positive experiences that Igbo people had with NduEru (as our Ezza people call the Aro) since the fifteenth century helped to evoke hatred, fear, and horror on the one hand, and wonder, awe, and admiration on the other.[1] As a result of the kidnapping of Olauda and countless other victims during the period, it is still a taboo for any indigenous Ezza

---

1   Ndu Life Njoku, The Dual Image of the Aro –JORA 2015

man or woman to marry an Arochukwu person. However, in the advent of colonial Christianity, things seem to be changing.

3

EPIC NARRATIVE

Ndubisi: Life first before anything else

"In the first expressions of my grief I reproached my *fate* and wished I had never been born. I was ready to curse the tide that bore us, the gale that wafted my prison, and even the ship that conducted us; and I called on death to relieve me from the horrors I felt and dreaded, that I might be in that place." [2]

In 1788, Olauda, my Igbo kinsman wrote what many people consider as the first and most important book ever written by a slave. The book *The Interesting Narrative of the Life of Olaudah Equiano (Olauda Ikwueno or Gustavus Vassa, the African* became not only a historical record of survival but also a protest against slavery. As one of the earliest anti-slavery books ever written, *The Interesting Narrative* has been recognized as the turning point in the campaign which influenced the British parliament

---

2   p.88 The Interesting Narrative...edited by Robert. J. Allison 1995 Bedford Books, Boston.

to abolish slavery and the USA to enact the *Emancipation Proclamation.*

But most importantly, the book is the first written history of the Igbo ethnic nation from the 17th century. Most of other African people are not so privileged to document their oral history like Olauda did. The Igbo ethnic nation has gone through many transitions: In 1914, the British colonial ruler named Fredrick Lord Lugard amalgamated southern and northern protectorates into the political creature known as Nigeria. On October 1, 1960, Nigeria declared it's independence from the British Empire. On May 30, 1967, the ethnic Igbo nation declared it's independence from Nigeria resulting into a 3-year war between Nigeria and the newly created Nation State. Since January 1970, the Republic of Biafra which existed and recognized by 11 countries has been under captivity after Nigeria defeated the new Nation and annexed it to the Nigerian Federation.

As Igbo people, we have been suffering from identity crisis since Olauda's enslavement. Under colonial rule, we were known as British protected citizens. After Nigeria's independence, we became Nigerian citizens. For 3 years, we existed in freedom as Biafran citizens and as vanquished Biafran people, we became Nigerian citizens again. After 50 years under Nigerian rule, the Biafran people are still fighting for their freedom.

4

OUR CURRENT CONDITION

Ndukaku: Life is greater than wealth

The president of the United States loses re-election and instigates a mob leading to violence and destruction of lives and property at the US Congress. Five lives are lost.

- A policeman kneels on an African American man's neck for 8 minutes and squeezes life out of him. George Floyd dies.
- A policeman pumps bullets into a black woman's home. Breonna Taylor dies.
- Africans show indifference to the condition of African Americans. Lives are lost.

For a deeper understanding of what we sometimes naively call *injustice* or historical wrongdoing let us work with the hypothesis that in every evil behavior there must be a reckoning according to Olauda's ethnic Ezza doctrine and ideology.

Questions arise, should the perpetrator of slavery be regarded by society as a danger to be stopped or a psychiatrist patient to be treated? If so, why is the US Constitution not protective of African Americans?

On the contrary, does a slave master or government owe a debt to be paid to descendants of the enslaved Africans? Is the payment of reparation by present day Americans not a form of creating new zones of injustice against innocent people who are being punished for the sins of their ancestors? Olauda and African Americans have become the visible symbols of the *Inweronye* constituency – the less-privileged humanity. Both the African Americans and the continental Africans which Olauda represents are still treated as the illegitimate constituency – 'of a kind similar to but inferior.'

The drama of wrongdoing and retributive justice continue to fascinate the human mind. In humanity's quest for *Uwaoma* – the great and virtuous society, there is a consensus that Karma is real.

In most civilized societies, it is the constitutional duty of political leaders, police and courts to maintain law and order and to punish crime. 'For, how long shall the ungodly triumph.' On the contrary, should the politician who incites mob insurrection and the police that kneels on black necks or breaks into a sleeping black woman's home and murders her be considered as perpetrators or psychiatric patients to be treated? However, according to Amaechina, there is another long-forgotten perspective in dealing with this unfinished reparation wahala - dilemma.

5

AMAECHINA'S LAST LETTER

Evolution and the making of the Life of Nobody.
Amaechina – May our home never vanish and become a
forest

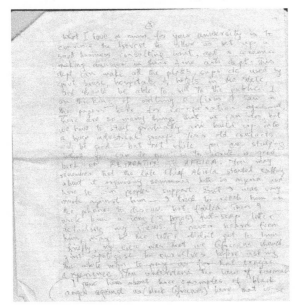

On May 14, 2000, Humphrey Amaechina wrote me what would become his last letter. Humphrey was a *Higher*

Initiate of Eckankar - the religion of the Light and Sound of God. In the letter, he instructs, "What you can do, (but not when you are studying) is to write a good book on REPARATION TO AFRICA. In his final words he suggests, "We Africans should first apologize to ourselves before asking the white man to pay us for that tragic experience [because] the law of karma is strong." Horowitz, the dialectical thinker, contends:

"Yes, but what does this even mean? That he, Humphrey, should apologize to himself? That you [Ewa] should apologize to yourself? The implication of his statement is not clear."

Ewa: "What Humphrey means is none of the above. He simply wants continental Africans to apologize to their African American relatives and other Black diasporic people for their ancestors' (Aro slave traders) culpability in the human rights abuses of fellow Africans sold into slavery."

Who is Nathaniel Horowitz?

Nathaniel Horowitz and Ewa Unoke
Covid-19 era: StayingSafe

I think it is appropriate now to introduce my dialectical opponent whom I had earlier called an interlocutor. As an American Irishman-Jew, Nat likes to play the devil's advocate. In the search for truth, which is at the center of our discourses, Horowitz most times holds a uniquely different point of view on the reparation questions I raise from an Africanworld's viewpoint. As a reasoned debate between the African and American perspectives, both Horowitz and I, no doubt, have a common goal: to examine the issue of reparation from multiple perspectives to establish the *truth* about the unresolved 'injustice' of slavery. As the book's subtitle indicates, I will now explain the subaltern theory of *Inweronye?*

Inweronye is an Ezza (Igbo) word which speaks to how the powerful politician arrogantly interrogates the poor and long excluded society "Who do you have? Why should I not deal with you or ignore you. You are a non-person." Inweronye has no representation in government. The politicians who ought to represent Inweronye are usually corrupt and flamboyant. Therefore, Onweonye, the politically excluded citizen and his society have nobody to fight for them, and nobody to represent and protect them. Inweronye is another name for the subaltern – the lowest rank of humanity. From the slave era until now, what perpetrator-countries and governments seem to be saying to the African Americans is this - *Your life is the life of nobody* just like Olauda, the bastard child of humanity who was born free but remained in shackles everywhere he turned for over 10 years as a slave.

Nwokorom (a fond nickname for my closest friends) Alphonsus Ibeogu named his thriving law firm *Inweronye Chambers.* His primary objective was to defend *onweonye* - the poor and voiceless humanity who had no tree to lean on. When the military Governor of Enugu State nominated him for the position of State Attorney General, he declined the offer. Both of us had figured out that his legal counsel and services to our long-forgotten *wawa* (long-exploited) society would find him irreplaceable. However, *Nwokorom* Ibeogu aka "Pontus" was assassinated before we could discuss the case of our Igbo kinsman, Olauda. I could not ask him the very obvious question "What is justice for our Ezza homeboy, Olauda?"

Now, even for running the risk of repeating my story, one of the unfinished *injustices* of the *trans-Atlantic slave trade* is the story of my homeboy, Olauda Ikwueno. In our Ezza dialect, Olauda means *precious loud jewel* while Ikwueno *means the fourth kindred.* Both Olauda's first and last names were wrongly pronounced and mis-spelled as Olaudah Equiano. Today, there exists a kindred community in Ezza South Local Government named Ikwueto, meaning *the third kindred.* Nobody knows what really happened to Ikwueno, the fourth kindred – Olauda's name.

Igbo Indifference

Why is the Igbo society so indifferent to slavery and reparation, especially, when the largest number of enslaved Africans were allegedly Ndigbo? What is justice for Olauda and his ethnic Igbo nation regardless of the often-skewed data used to validate parochial research. While Ezza Kamenuists believe that no amount of dollar payment can "repair" the cultural, economic and spiritual damages done by perpetrators, the American civil rights movement clashes with the African point of view - spiritual justice. While the mystic's theory seeks to reconcile humanity's karma and heal the past, on the contrary, reparation advocates seek only economic justice. With this clash between the two contending transitional justice approaches, what is the right justice for Africa? What is justice for Olauda and his long-exploited Igbo nation?

In the 21st century, what does the post-slavery society need most on its long transition towards recovery, healing and reconciliation? As history and experience reveal, there is no degree of realpolitik (power politics) or use-of-force that can contain *Black Anger* and now, White Rage worldwide until society and government understand the root causes of *Black*

Anger and *White Rage*. While the African Diaspora seeks reparation in reckoning with their unpleasant past, their continental (Igbo) relatives deal with the injustices of slavery by invoking on the natural law of karma to avenge for them.

6

KARMA IS REAL

Kamenu: We reap what we sow in life

Slavery was not new to Olauda. His father owned slaves. Olauda had always the premonition that one day he would be kidnapped according to his own personal testimonies. Kamenuists – the seekers of deeper truth and honesty believe that understanding how karma works in our lives could liberate us from our past and present victim-oriented mentality. When we open our *third eyes* or spiritual eyes, the Kamenuist assures us, we would begin, to gain deeper insights and deeper underpinnings of our so-called injustices. When our spiritual eyes open, our historical injustices would melt away into greater opportunities for our growth.

Kamenuism – as an ideology is the way of life of the Ezza people. We are seekers of truth and virtuous life. An adherent considers himself a free spirit, dogma-free and pathless spirituality. They practice Ezza freedom theology of cause-and-effect. Kamenuists do not believe in the concept of sin.

They refuse to be called sinners since in Ezza social teaching, a sinner is seen as an outcast or a criminal. Olauda and his sisters' ordeal was not a coincidence. Rather, it was the law of cause-and-effect in action. Most times, we reap what we sow through our acts of commission and omission – what we did directly or what we failed to do. In this physical universe, we carry two karmic loads as credit and debit on our shoulders every moment of our existence. When we enslave someone's children, our own children would suffer the same fate. Ancient Ezza sages like the Kamenuists were seekers and not believers. The law of karma requires the seekers to follow the highest code of ethics.

According to Robert J. Allison, slavery not only deprived Equiano of his freedom but cut him off from the Igbo spiritual universe. p.5 [3]

Boomerang Effect

Let me repeat: The secret to healing from the past and present injustices is to understand the law of Kamenu. The Orientals call it karma. Karma, most times, controls our lives in this world. Our actions have boomerang effects, whether we believe it or not, we usually reap what we sowed in life. When we know how this law works, we would learn to 'burn' the karma or the so-called injustices in this world. The core elements of Kamenuism are:

- Law of karma is real.
- An adherent is a free spirit.
- Ezza liberation theology.
- Non-dogmatic.
- Pathless route to God.

---

3   Robert J. Allison, Igbo spiritual universe. p.5.

- Seekers of divine truth and honesty.
- Adherents have no concept of sin.
- But they are conscious that people reap what they sow.
- Kamenuists do not pay church dues.
- Kamenuists have no "Holy Book."
- They do not claim to have seen God but they believe that God is not a man.
- They believe there are so many paths that lead to God.
- They are not afraid to follow their ancestral spiritual original path.

Ezza Spiritual Atonement

During my childhood, I witnessed secret rituals performed annually by the oldest men in my *Adakaogu* (warrior chimp) family. Just before the ceremony began, women and children were forced to lock themselves up in their grass huts. It was an abomination for them to catch a glimpse of the atonement ceremony. Although men did not cook in Ezza villages, the old men would assemble at the entrance of my grandfather's residence, remove their *anuma* (waist towels) and peel yams, strangle a cock, prepare yam porridge and invoke a particular spirit to join them. At the end of the ceremony, the men would chant, pour libation before having a cleansing bath to enable them to metaphorically return from (astral) the spirit world to the physical universe purified.

The purpose of the ritual was to appease or to make peace and reconcile with an unknown relative who was kidnapped and never returned during the slavery period. Since then, there have been dreams and signs that the wandering spirit of this unknown relative is restless and angry. When this happens, our family begins to slide into various fortuitous mishaps like accidents, untimely death, sickness, poverty and more. Sometimes there would be death dreams that threatened the survival and happiness of our family.

To us, as descendants of the greatest Ezza warrior kindreds, we are constantly asking Chineke (Igbo Creation God) and our nameless relative to forgive us. If we refuse to atone for our ancestral Kamenu or karma, then we are doomed to suffer unimaginable misery.

Ironically, while the African indigenous nations believe in restorative justice and karma, Europe and America remain indifferent to Karma – the law of cause and effect – like the proverbial man who is busy chasing rats while his house is on fire.

"Dignity and justice for all of us"- cries out Olauda.

"I wept very bitterly for some time: and began to think I must have done something to displease the Lord that he thus punished me so severely. This filled me with painful reflections on my past conduct." Olauda p.86.[4]

Kidnapped by our own Igbo "countrymen" and enslaved in the Americas and Europe, millions of Igbo indigenous citizens were kidnapped, sold into slavery and treated like bastards – the illegitimate children of nobody. In rethinking the trans-Atlantic slave trade, 187 years after Britain abolished slavery and 157 years after Lincoln's emancipation of the African slaves, the world remains indifferent to paying reparation to descendants of victims.

---

4   Olauda p.86.

But it's an issue whose time has arrived. Reparation will be paid in this our lifetime.

7

CONTENDING THEORIES OF REPARATION

Atula Egwu: Do not be afraid
(Harcourt Wyte the Leprosy Patient and Poet)

Africans at home and in diaspora are still in transition from the dark history of slavery. The United States fought a Civil War, and when postwar peace occurred decades later, the society and government abandoned the efforts to seek justice and reparation for the enslaved victims. For over a century, postwar reconstruction was based on *victor's justice* and remains so today. On the contrary, Nathaniel Horowitz (my dependable critic) argues that "The federal government was hampered in its attempts to bring some justice to the formerly-enslaved African-Americans by the southern whites who clung to their power by mostly-illegal means."

In West Africa, the ancestral home of most of the enslaved Africans, the emphasis on reckoning with the past is not on justice and monetary compensation. Rather, Africans are more concerned with the future and the need for moral reconstruction after the evil of slavery. While the African American descendants seek compensation, punishment, and reconciliation according to the law, their African relatives are, ironically, sitting at a separate table.

Institutional slavery in the African world (Africa, Caribbean, the Americas, and Europe) is an unfinished business. Africans, rightly or wrongly, believe that there is Karma at work in the cards life has dealt us. Based on the two contending viewpoints on reparation, my aim in this book is to close the vacuum created by Africa's indifference to the past and present human rights abuses and the reparation debate. I am, therefore on a perilous crusade to exhume and re-examine Olauda and his *Interesting Narrative*. As Olauda's relative (fellow Igbo), my updated story of our homeland will hopefully be refreshing to readers. But above all, most African youth might never have heard about Olauda or the Igbo ethnic nation and their ultra-democratic ideology. Finally, as a former victim, I shine light on this human dilemma in order to minimize or to end the scourge of child kidnapping.

Over 40 million people worldwide are still enslaved. "Human trafficking is modern day slavery and it occurs when one person uses manipulation, threats and/or violence to control another person in order to take advantage of them for economic gain."[5]

This upgraded story of Olauda is a reliable contribution to the current debate on reparation. His story as a survivor represents the untold stories of the countless Igbo victims, especially, the Ezza ethnic slaves who did not survive.

---

5   Mark Tutton, CNN, 09/ 20, 2017.

8

BLOOD GUILT

The Danger of Imagining Others
"Father, you like me as I am (leprosy patient).
Therefore, I do not worry."
Harcourt Wyte.

Nick Berg, a 29-year-old Jewish American freelance radio-tower repairman, was kidnapped and beheaded in Iraq. A video of this act was released in May 2004 by Islamist militants who said they were acting in response to the Abu Ghraib torture and prisoner abuse by the United States military of Iraqi prisoners.

On the night of April 15, 2014, 276 female students were kidnapped from their Secondary School in Chibok, Borno State, Nigeria. Responsibility for the kidnappings was claimed by Boko Haram, an Islamist militant group which believes that western education is evil.

In 1968, at the age of 12, I was kidnapped, tortured, and imprisoned by Muslim soldiers of the Nigerian Army at St. Paul's Primary School, Amudo, Ezza. After spending one night at the makeshift Abaomege jail, we were transported to Abakaliki maximum security prison. After my brave father negotiated my release, I came to the conclusion that in life, it is better to die fighting for freedom than be kidnapped and beheaded as a bloody civilian. I voluntarily joined the Biafran Organization of Freedom Fighters – BOFF.

What is common in the stories of Nick Berg, the Chibok girls, and me is that we were all victims of kidnapping. To be able to abduct and harm their victims, the perpetrators would, first, imagine us as enemies, as evil, as objects, and as infidels, who must be purged out of the society. Our kidnappers imagined our lives as the lives of nobodies. To be able to murder Nick Berg, his murderers would have to *imagine* him as an American Jew. 'Americans are evil. Americans are our enemies. Therefore, society must be purged of the Americans.' This difficulty of imagining others who are different from us is the root cause of the danger we face today. This *danger of imagining others* is quite evident politically, economically and religiously in our past and present polarized world. The Aro (Igbo kidnappers), Americans and Europeans who kidnapped, bought and sold their fellow human beings as commodities were all entangled in this moral dilemma - karma.

In our practice of democracy, sometimes, we imagine our ideological opponents as enemies who should not only be defeated but, if possible, eliminated. Most of us are guilty of the difficulty of imagining others who are different from us, whether they are Black, Caucasian, Spanish, Igbo, Jewish, Gay, Lesbian, Conservative, Liberal, Poor, Rich, Christian or Muslim. The danger is real. From one generation to another, researchers and students have continued their relentless search for more facts about the life and times of *Olaudah Equiano*, also known as *Gustavus Vassa, the African.*

As his kinsman, I have observed many misrepresentations and distortions of facts in the plethora of literature on his life. In the current debate, Olauda's story would be used as a case study to represent the millions of Igbo people and other West Africans sold and enslaved in the new world. Most importantly, Olauda represents the millions of Igbo men and women whose names have been permanently lost in captivity. The question then becomes, who has the right to speak for the dead victims? Can reparative justice cleanse the blood guilt of all those who were involved in institutional slavery?

9

A LIFE OPENED

Ndi Uwaoma Kelenu Chineke Unu: Those who are blessed in this world, give praise to God.
In my own cursed world, I will also give praise and thanks to God.
Those of you who are like me, whose morning Sun has refused to shine, have patience.
Atula egwu, man, woman, child do not be afraid because,
the God who leads you is the greatest warrior in your battle.
Harcourt Wyte.

Olauda was an ordinary Igbo citizen who lived an extraordinary life. In the Igbo language, *Olauda* means "loud and precious metal." His father's name was Ikwueno, meaning in our Ezza language is "the fourth kindred." Olauda Ikwueno, wrongly spelled *Olaudah Equiano* or Gustavus Vassa, was one of my fellow Igbos who were kidnapped, shipped across the Atlantic Ocean and enslaved. After Olauda had been enslaved for over 30 years his abolitionist movement helped to end slavery in Europe. According to his narrative, Olauda was born around 1745. From his name, culture, history, geography, occupation and vivid description of his place of birth, it is strongly believed that Olauda was an Ezza, Abakaliki teenager from what is now the Ebonyi State in Nigeria. Kidnapped from his Igbo village at the age of 11 along with his sister, Olauda writes in his autobiography,

"I believe there are a few events in my life which have not happened to many."

According to Olauda's narrative, "Slavery is when the law allows one person to own another like a piece of property. Slave owners can make that person do whatever they want. Slaves have no human rights. They work under very harsh conditions and can be bought and sold."

Slavery is an ancient custom. Virtually all ancient and modern societies practiced or still practice one form of slavery or another, including, especially, ancient Greece, Egypt, Rome, and African nations.

Perpetrators

Between the 15th and 16th centuries, European traders from Britain, Netherlands, France, Portugal and Spain explored the coasts of West Africa, especially the Bights of Benin and Biafra, looking for people to buy and sell as slaves. "These people were then shipped to the colonies of America and the Caribbean to work as slave labour." Equiano ibid p. 5.[6]

---

6   Equiano ibid p. 5.

The Middle Passage

The Middle Passage is the journey of the slave ships from West Africa across the Atlantic Ocean to America. Usually, such ships were fully loaded with the enslaved Africans. Many of these Africans died from disease, malnutrition, or other mistreatment, and would never reach the New World. In the 21st century, who has the right to speak for the African victims? Those at home or those in the Diaspora? Africans, African Americans or Caribbean people?

10

TRANSITIONAL JUSTICE

Tochukwu – Give praise and thanks to God.

The theoretical framework of this book is transitional justice. The theme of transitional justice speaks to how societies and governments deal with the injustices or wrongdoings of the past. Should the perpetrators of the trans-Atlantic slave trade be punished or pardoned? These questions become especially more important for societies making the transition from dictatorship to democracy. Germany following Nazism, South Africa after Apartheid, and democratization in Latin America and East-Central Europe, for example, Nigeria after prebendal politics. How do the Africans, African Americans and the Caribbean people deal with the unhealed past?

In the post - George Floyd era, how will the Biden-Harris government deal with reparation to the African American society and the African continent? Experts argue that transition towards durable peace must be based on the rule of law, truth, justice and reparation. When victims tell the truth, and governments do justice, then, society would reconcile towards peace and national recovery.

TRUTH

JUSTICE

RECONCILIATION

FUTURE

- *Truth*: our goal here is truth-telling in order to amend past misrepresentations
- *Justice*: asserting the right to accept or reject monetary compensation
- *Reconciliation*: establishing truth commissions, criminal courts, and Rwanda-style community-justice Gacaca courts
- *Future*: towards a culture of *ozo emena, nunca más*, never again.

However, people who contend or disagree with this theory raise the questions like how far, how many generations can demand this justice and reparation? How far can we pursue justice? The kidnapping of African men and women into slavery created a historic wrong. Opponents of transitional justice further argue that we cannot remedy the injustices of history. Igbo Kamenuists believe that religion is the answer to how post-conflict societies could remedy the injustices of the past. As the Biden-Harris government begins to re-examine the reparation question, it should examine the issue from many world views, such as;

- Reconciliation - Religious justice

- Punishment - Legal justice
- Kamenu or Karma - Natural justice

In dealing with reparation to the victims, government and society should understand that there is religious value in transitional justice as well as legal value when resolving this complex issue. There are also old traditional precedents and values, example, the trial and execution of King Charles I of England and Louis XVI King of France.

Dialectics of Reparative Justice

No doubt, the question of reparation has an endless fascination for humanity. From ancient Chinese, Greeks, Africans, and everyone else, it remains a central theme in the world's quest for peace and happiness.

How should the slave master, government and society be treated? Should capital punishment be meted out to perpetrators and murderers of slaves posthumously? To what extent should ignorance exempt them from punishment and reparation? These questions are both legal and political in nature; they concern both the jurist and statesman. But above all, they are questions of right and wrong.

Should present-day slave-holding individuals be regarded as enemies to be crushed? Should those of the past be regarded as debtors who must be persuaded to pay monetary compensation to slave descendants? Can society and government dismiss these moral issues simply as inconsequential truths? Advocates of utilitarianism like Jeremy Bentham will argue that the pain of the perpetrator is an evil as the victim's pain is, when society considers punishing evildoers or seeking reparations or to making atonement for wrongdoing. In order words, punishment is like committing another evil.

As a Kamenuist, I believe in healing and reconciliation. However, many seekers are aware that no human court or Truth Commission can correctly assess moral guilt, and no punishment can compensate enough for it. Similarly, reparation is immeasurable in respect of the amount of money commensurate with the amount of pain actually suffered.

The popular perspective holds that criminal justice should have two purposes, deterrence and reformation of criminal offenders. But can human justice ensure that reparation is proportionate to the crime of slavery committed? The Book of Exodus stipulates charging "an eye for an eye, a tooth for a tooth." But when no body parts are directly in play, how can we guarantee that reparative justice ensures that the compensation is not more and not less than the original damage done? Shakespeare's *Merchant of Venice* debacle is a reminder of the difficulty of demanding a perpetrator's *pound of flesh*.

Kamenu vs Ochichi: Natural Justice vs. Power Politics

There is a difference between the two groups above. While the Kamenuist represents the old school of natural justice, the advocates of modern power politics, also known as *Ochichi*, believe in the use of force. From that perspective, the primary concern is to prevent the crime of slavery now and in the future, or, at least, to minimize the evil of modern-day slavery in any form or shape. However, believers in Kamenu know the superiority of karma or natural justice – the concept that we reap what we sow in life.

Reparation is one of the transitional justice tools at the disposal of the contemporary Ochichi (ruler or leader). It is neither the best nor the most effective. TJ can be very expensive. However, governments and societies can use this mechanism if they cannot find a cheaper one. Furthermore, it is common sense that society should not seek reparation in anger but should wait until one has cooled down. Transition towards durable peace must be based on karmic truth, justice and reparation and not on the rule of guns and swords.

As the Ochichi advocates see it, crime must be punished. If government pardons a criminal perpetrator of violence, the guilt falls on Ndi Ochichi, the political leaders or rulers.

In summary, Ndi Ochichi suggest that the criminal wrong of slavery is a national debt. And such a debt is something which governments, societies and victims cannot ignore. Somehow, in a well-organized political society, a debt of property, money, or life must be paid. In the Ezza society, to ask for payment may be a mark of respect or redemption to the debtor. It is to be assumed that the debtor or perpetrator is a responsible and honorable person who is prepared to meet his liabilities.

Race to Undo the Past

In the USA, the theme of reparation for slavery has come up often in moral, religious and political discussions since at least the time of Abraham Lincoln's *Emancipation Proclamation*.

During the trans-Atlantic slave trade, a criminal compensation was incurred, which ought to be paid. In other words, an evil act was committed which must be atoned for. Put another way, damage was done and ought to be repaired; a sin was committed which must be atoned for; an evil precedent had been set which must be cancelled. These transitional justice metaphors are quite universal. The demand for reparation is usually linked with a craving to undo the past. Somehow, in most cases, both the perpetrators and the victims wish for reparative justice to annul or wipe out the injustice. "To the one it brings a sense of satisfaction, to the other a sense of expiation."[7]

"Is the whole idea of reparation not an obvious delusion?" asks the Kamenuist. "A game may be replayed, and a debt maybe cancelled; these things are superficial. But when we quit poetry for prose and come to the realities of moral life, is not any notion of reparation a pure absurdity?" It is inconceivable to see how a moral wrong can be wiped out by monetary compensation.

If one man robs another of his car, the obvious way to rectify the injustice is to require the criminal offender to return the stolen car to its rightful owner. Sometimes, such restitution may not be possible, especially if the stolen goods no longer exist. In this case, the culprit will be required to give not only compensation for the stolen goods but also damages for the loss of the opportunity to use them.

But what happens when the damage is done to the person and not his property? It is estimated that over 1.4 million indigenous Igbo people were transported in European ships across the Atlantic Ocean during the slavery era.[8] Most of the enslaved men and women came from Ezza Igbo sub-ethnic nation of West Africa – my homeland.

---

7   Ibid p.186.
8   *By Adaobi Tricia Nwaubani* Updated Sept. 20, 2019.

11

EKE

Ometaru Vuru – Whatever you sow, you'll reap.

Olauda did not want to become a diplomat or traveler. But his course was determined by his akalaka (providence). Others would control his destiny. "The market [Eke Ezza] in his Igbo village drew people from all over southeastern Nigeria coming to trade for Ezza cotton, corn and yams. From the south, Aro traders brought European goods: guns, cloth, and hats. The Aros also traded slaves."

Recall that one day, when the adults were at work, in their (farms) three Aro traders snatched [Olauda] and his sister, put them in a large sack (Ezza people call the large bag ekpa nkpuru) and carried them away. Who has the right to seek reparation for Olauda, his sister, and Ezza parents?

The Eke market, which still exists today, was the largest market for selling and buying slaves during the 15th, 16th and 17th centuries when Olauda and his sister were kidnapped from their Ezza village and sold. For quite obvious reasons, Olauda is likely an Ezza indigene from Ntsokara village. His typical Ezza name, Olauda, means the precious son born to be popular. His father's name, Ikwueno, translates to the fourth kindred. Indigenes of the brotherly ethnic nations of Ezza, Ikwo and Izzi are collectively known as Abakaliki. From ancient to modern times, the Abakaliki community has been known as the food-basket of West Africa. According to commentators on his Narrative, "Though Olaudah never saw a white person until he reached the African [Calabar] coast, his village was tied to the Atlantic economy. The market women traded iron pots and European cloth for their baskets, perfumes, dyes, and crops. His village also raised corn and tobacco, which had been grown only in America before 1492...." Olauda ibid.

The first people of Igbo ancestry were brought to the United States by force through the port city of Calabar. The enslaved Igbo people suffered grave physical injuries through the slave masters' malicious intents and actions. In this case, the only possible compensation is indeed not *in pari material*, not comparable, with the wrongdoing. Although lawyers could work out an estimated cost to repair such damage, in a deeper reality beyond the superficial level, the status quo cannot be restored. No financial payments, whether $5,000 or $50,000 or $500,000,000, can return a life or a limb. Such a reparation is only a consolatory payment which cannot restore the arm, the leg, or the life lost.

Religion

Igbo people prefer spiritual well-being to material well-being. Is it any wonder that in captivity, Olauda, at the peak of his suffering, felt that fate's darkest clouds were gathering over his head?

Slavery not only deprived him his freedom, but also alienated him from the spiritual universe of his homeland. When Olauda thought his moment of freedom was near, he was resold to a Quaker named Robert King. "I wept very bitterly for some time: and began to think I must have done something to displease the Lord, that he thus punished me so severely... In the first expression of my grief, I reproached my fate and wished I had never been born. I was ready to curse the tide that bore us, the gale that wafted my prison and even the ship that conducted us; and I called on death to relieve me from the horrors I felt and dreaded that I might be in that place.... I called upon God's thunder and his avenging power to direct the stroke of death to me rather than permit me to become a slave, and to be sold from lord to lord."

Law of Kamenu

Even the fullest compensation to Ndigbo (Igbo people), the worst victims of the trans-Atlantic slave trade, can only appear on the surface to annul the wrong done during the era. The wrongdoing in which Ndigbo, Europeans, and Americans were culpable constitute not only crimes of tort or civil wrong, but, more importantly, are regarded as crimes against humanity. If indeed this is true, then there is no amount of monetary compensation that can cleanse or wipe out the crimes and injustices of slavery. Payments cannot reverse the crime.

From a Kamenuist worldview, there is no amount of atonement that a murderer makes which can make something else out of him other than a murderer. In Kamenuist law, it is a delusion for the criminal offender to think about forgiveness of sins. Kamenuist do not believe in the concept of "sin." What Ezza people regard as sin is for example, a murderer or a witch or an evil person. Ordinary innocent citizens do not belong to the above category. Ezza people reject anybody calling them sinners because this means anyone so labeled is wicked and as such a threat to community peace and security – hence, such a person must be eliminated from the community. In Kamenu, a deeper reality, what is done is done. What is done cannot be undone. An evil man remains an evil man until he recreates himself, despite any form or shape of reparation or expiation he may make or suffer."[9]

Today, the wound of slavery has left an unhealed scar which still hurts society in many new ways. Can reparative justice annul historical wrongdoings? It is doubtful. We live in a period of political infidelity. Those who campaign for reparation believe they have a moral obligation to do so. Their goal is to punish the historical injustice of slavery. However, to the critics, seeking to remedy past wrongdoing is irrational. It does not matter whether you are a realist, idealist, or Kamenuist, Olauda's narrative is an important contribution in working out a moral estimate of the wrongs done to Igbo people. The root cause of the Igbo Curse, Igbo bondage and suffering in Nigeria today is undoubtedly linked to the unhealed past.

Ndigbo have not collectively atoned for their complicity in the trans-Atlantic slave trade. As a Kamenuist, I want to state without mincing words that Aro people are both perpetrators and victims of the trans-Atlantic commodification of human beings for profit purposes.

The question further arises whether or not the descendants of the enslaved victims are also victims? This is not a topic that has been settled to everyone's satisfaction and needs to be stated explicitly. A very common conservative idea here in the USA is that black people have done better in the USA than they would

---

9   ibid p.190.

have done had their ancestors not been taken into slavery. In other words, the condition of African Americans is better than that of Igbos and their African kinsmen and women.

It is absurd to think that monetary compensation can wipe out the bloodguilt of the perpetrators of slavery. I do not necessarily object to the notion of reparation if governments, societies, and victims can agree. However, my contention is that what is done in slavery is done and cannot be undone through reparative justice.

My friend, Horowitz disagrees.

"I'm not sure what your point is. Nobody is saying that what is done can be undone. It can only be compensated for. If everyone involved agrees on compensation, what is the problem? The only problem I can see is that not everyone involved is going to agree on a just compensation. And the neo-Nazis in the USA will want compensation for their indentured European Irish ancestors."

12

HUMAN RIGHTS TODAY

*Echi Di Ime – Tomorrow is pregnant – Tomorrow is
unpredictable.*

What I mean is that transition to a more durable security
must be based on truth, justice, and reparation.
Truthtelling can establish the facts about the violations of
human rights that occurred in the past, for example during the
trans-Atlantic slave trade. Transitional justice seeks to restore
the victims' rights, to reject impunity, to pardon or to punish,
and to seek apology. Meanwhile, reparation provides various
forms of compensation for the victims. There is a need to seek
guarantee of non-repetition of such abuses in the future. There
is also a need for documentation in order to say, *Never Again,
Ozoemena and Nunca Mas.*

Currently, some 40 million people are victims of modern-
day slavery.

- 25 million people in forced labor

- 15 million people in forced marriage
- Women and girls account for 71% of the victims
- Children account for 25% [10]

Reparation activists argue that modern slavery is a greater threat to global peace and security than the reparation issue, which is like living in the past. To overcome it is painful and recent violent right-wing insurrection, activists, victims and sympathizers must in reality solve the problem of human right abuses in the past and in the present, according to Shakespeare, the past is a prologue.

Trans-Atlantic Slave Trade Data

Number of Slaves Transported by Each European Country

Country	Voyages	Slaves Transported
Portugal (including Brazil)	30,000	4,650,000
Spain (including Cuba)	4,000	1,600,000
France (including West Indies)	4,200	1,250,000
Holland	2,000	500,000
Britain	12,000	2,600,000
British North America, U.S.A	1,500	300,000
Denmark	250	50,000
Other	250	50,000
Total	**54,200**	**11,000,000**[11]

Reparation activists counter argue that the injustices of the trans-Atlantic slave trade are too monumental in human, economic and spiritual toll to be ignored.

Number of Slaves Delivered to Each Country/Destination

10   https://news.un.org/en/story/2018/12/1027271.
11   http://www.slaverysite.com/Body/facts%20and%20figures.htm.

Country / Destination	Slaves Delivered	%
Brazil	4,000,000	35.3
Spanish Empire (including Cuba)	2,500,000	22.1
British West Indies	2,000,000	17.7
French West Indies (including Cayenne)	1,600,000	14.1
British North America & U.S.	500,000	4.4
Dutch West Indies (including Surinam)	500,000	4.4
Danish West Indies	28,000	0.2
Europe (including Portugal, Canary Islands, Madeira, Azores, etc.)	200,000	1.8
Total	**11,328,000**	**100**[12]

Number of Slaves Leaving African Ports

African Port	Number of Slaves Departing	%
Senegambia (including Arguin, Sierra Leone)	2,000,000	15.4
Windward Coast	250,000	1.9
Ivory Coast	250,000	1.9
Gold Coast (Ashanti)	1,500,000	11.5
Slave Coast (Dahomey, Adra, Oyo)	2,000,000	15.4
Benin to Calabar	2,000,000	15.4
Cameroons / Gabon	250,000	1.9
Loango	750,000	5.8
Congo / Angola	3,000,000	23.1
Mozambique / Madagascar	1,000,000	7.7
Total Leaving African Ports[13]	**13,000,000**	**100**

---

12   http://www.slaverysite.com/Body/facts%20and%20figures.htm.
13   http://www.slaverysite.com/Body/facts%20 and%20figures.htm.

"According to these statistics, you're wrong that most of the enslaved people came from Igbo land," Horowitz argues against my earlier statement.

Ewa: *Slavery.com* compiled the above data from only one source. For a better understanding of why Igbo people were the most enslaved victims, let us take a more comprehensive look at the state and nature of the Igbo slavery and why their case is different from others.

The Igbo, whose traditional territory is called the Bight of Biafra (also known as the Bight of Bonny), became one of the principal ethnic groups to be enslaved during the Trans-Atlantic Slave Trade. An estimated 14.6% of all slaves were taken from the Bight of Biafra between 1650 and 1900. The Bight's major slave trading ports were located in Bonny and Calabar.[3] The majority of Igbo slaves were kidnapped during village raids. The journey for Igbo slaves often began in the ancient Oracle known as Ibiniukpabi Temple located in Arochukwu Kingdom. [4] Gradually, Europeans began to encroach on Igbo territory, thus causing the kingdoms to desire weaponry to defend themselves. In order to obtain European goods and weaponry, Arochukwu began to raid villages of the other Igbo kingdoms - primarily those located in the Igbo hinterlands. People would be captured, regardless of gender, social status, or age. Slaves could have been originally farmers, nobility, or even people who had committed petty crimes. These captured slaves would be taken and sold to the British on the coast. Another way people were enslaved was through the divine oracle which resided in the Cave Temple complex. [6] All Igbos practiced divination called Afa, but the Kingdom of Arochukwu was different because it was headed by a divine oracle which was in charge of making decisions for the king.

During this time, if someone committed a crime, was in debt, or did something considered an "abomination" (for example, the killing of certain kinds of animals was considered an abomination due to its association with certain deities), they would be taken to the cave complex to face the oracle for sentencing. The oracle, which was also influenced by the British, would sentence these people to slavery, even for small crimes. The victim would be commanded to walk farther into the cave so that the spirits could "devour" them, but, in reality, they were taken to an opening on the other side and loaded directly onto a waiting boat. This boat would take them to a slave ship en route to the Americas[14].

14   14. Source:https://en.wikipedia.org/wiki/Igbo_people_in_the_Atlantic_slave_trade.

13

THEY DIED

Onwu ama Eze: Death knows no king,
knows no rich or poor and takes no bribe.

Slavery stripped the Africans of their identity and *they died.*
They died during the voyage.
Those who resisted were chained, they died.
Those who were jettisoned, died.
On the plantations. they died.
From the master's whip, they bled and died.
Not only death on the physical realm.
But death of dignity too.
Death of culture.
They were forced to take on new identities, new names, new
self, therefore, their family cultures and names died.
When their family life died, their children were
separated and sold.
Impacts today include violence, drug dealing and crime in the
black society.
Hence, we witnessed and read the runaway slave stories
exemplified by Harriet Tubman.

Take a trip to the African American museum you will see unimaginable imagery: photos of slaves with missing right toe, missing front teeth, this is what happened when they returned to their owners.

At the Savanna beaches, Georgia, Igbo slaves walked on water. From Williamsburg, VA to North and South Carolina, they died. From the slave revolutions of Haiti and the Maroons of Jamaica, they died.

From slave stories coming from St. Lucia (the Sarrots), Liverpool, and civil rights resulting to death, Malcolm X died; Martin Luther King JR died; Rosa Parks died.

This litany of African world deaths was compiled by Clementia Eugene, a friend and fellow Bison- (a graduate of Howard University).

Igbo: Long Walk to Freedom

"One day, when we had a smooth sea and moderate wind, two of my wearied [Igbo] countrymen who were chained together (I was near them at the time) preferring death to a life of misery, somehow made through the nettings and jumped into the sea: immediately, another quite dejected fellow ... followed their example." Ibid p.56[15] the Igbo journey towards regaining their freedom began from the trans-Atlantic-slave trade period ranging from the 15th-19th centuries. The European slave traders and the indigenous Aro from the Igbo ethnic nation imagined and commodified the abducted victims as mere chattels for economic gains and enrichment. After over three centuries, the Igbo ethnic nation is still fighting for their right to be free. It is difficult for a distant global community to feel the exclusion and misery of the caged Republic of Biafra nation in captivity.

---

15   Ibid p.56.

Black Lives Matter protesters

Protesting is a legitimate form of political participation, especially when law enforcement officers imagine the lives of a certain ethnic or racial group as the lives of non-persons. The picketing banner above reminds America that the life of a black man is a life of somebody, an mkparawa – a dignified gentleman.

14

NOVOTEL HOTEL LONDON

Onu kwube – Let the tongues wag.

On August 15, 2019, I arrived at Heathrow Airport, London with my friend, Professor Pamela Louis-Walden. As a surviving child soldier and former zonal commander of the Biafran Organization of Freedom Fighters (BOFF), I was invited as guest speaker during the genocide convention organized by the Indigenous Peoples of Biafra (IPOB) at the Goldsmith University of London. On the agenda also was my research plan to visit the graves of Olauda Ikwueno and his daughters; Anna Maria Vassa and Joanna Vassa, my Igbo relatives.

In 1792, Olauda married an English woman named Susanna Cullen and they lived in Cambridgeshire, England where they had two children – Anna Maria in 1793 and Joanna in 1795, it was a happy time for the couple. According to Paul Thomas and Victor Ambrus[16]. Olauda's first daughter Anna, died on

---

16   According to Paul Thomas and Victor Ambrus, the authors of Olaudah Equiano from

July 21, 1797 at the age of 4 years. Nothing much is known about Anna due to her early death.

In 1797, Joanna, the only surviving child of Olauda and Susanna Vassa, was just two years old when her mother died. It is speculated that her grandmother Anna Cullen raised her. During her time, Britain was going through social political unrest and most British women did not like the War. All they wanted to do was to get married. In June 1821, Henry Bromley was Ordained a minister at the Independent Chapel in Appledore, Devon. Two months after, Joanna married Henry at St James church in Clerkenwell, London. Joanna was 26 while Henry was 24.

Anna Maria Vassa

Joanna Vassa

On August 17, 2019, I visited Abney Park Cemetery in London, where Henry and Joanna were buried. Earlier, all my efforts to locate the grave of Olauda Equiano were unsuccessful. It is surprising why the grave of an Igbo prince and writer Olauda Ikwueno, who wrote a passionate account of the injustices of the trans-atlantic slave trade is secretly hidden somewhere in London. The explanation I got from Abney park rangers

slavery to freedom p.34, 2007. Published by Collins, London.

is that there is a clash of interest between the United States and Britain over the citizenship of Olauda. Both countries are claiming him as their citizen.

Sand and grass from Joanna's grave at Abney Park, London.
represents Olauda himself and his family.

As Olauda's fellow Igbo kinsman, I am dismayed to see the bushy and unkept graveside of Joanna and her husband Henry. I collected some of the overgrown grass and weed over her grave for a more dignified burial in Igboland. In Ezza culture, it is called "ajita maa" - exhuming and honouring the dead who had been lost for many years. Since there is so much speculation with regard to Olauda's immediate home in Africa, I have, on behalf of our Ancestors collected sand and weed from Joanna's grave for reburial at Ntsokara, Ezza in Ebonyi state on the same site which my Adakaogu Kinsmen have assigned me as the ruling prince and as the Ezeogo (current King) Ezza Ezekuna Worldwide.

Joanna Vassa and Henry

Professors Ewa Unoke and Pam Louis-Walden at Henry and Joannas' grave site at Abney Park, London.

On the second day, during a buffet breakfast at Novotel Hotels and Resorts, the unthinkable happened. Virtually all the seats and dining tables were occupied except one seat with a lonely British man in his early seventies. "Can I share the table with you?" I asked politely. After a brief hesitation, the man said, "Oh, yes, have a seat so you can serve me as my slave and get me as many cups of coffee as I want." I blacked out breathlessly. I went into a state of shock. When I recovered, I became angry.

I began to wonder: *How does one deal with a mis-educated Briton? Do I punch him in the face, spit on him or ignore him?* Then the wise words of Michelle Obama came tumbling into my head: "When they go low, we go high." What did I say to the British racist, "I do not think we still live in the age of palpable ignorance and empty arrogance. If we were still living in the dark ages of slavery, I think you could possibly have been my serf or slave as a poor and uneducated Briton since I am an Igbo prince and professor with a Ph.D." His response was pathetic "My daughter has a Ph.D." "There you are, we are not talking about your daughter..." I stretched out my hand to shake his hands after an unthinkable encounter. But my British cynic could not imagine a handshake with an African Kamenuist and free thinker.

Contrary to his wish, I sat down at the same table as my British nemesis, mischievously relishing his discomfort, thinking, *It's no more the slave era. Things have changed in London.* The enslaved people have paradoxically become more educated than the slave masters and their descendants. Afterwards, I photographed my British cynic.

The kidnapping of Olauda, my relative, during the 17th century and the recent attempt to enslave me by a British citizen illustrate vividly the difficulty of imagining others who are different from us by race, ideology, or gender. My aspiring "master," like his predecessors, could not imagine me as a person, a Ph.D. holder, a professor, an honest Igbo prince (first born male child) and Ezeogo. Rather, to the cynic, I am merely a non-person, a sub-human, a piece of property. My British antagonist reminded me that Donald Trump had asked the Africans in America to go back to their African huts. Although slavery was abolished in England about 250 years ago, my Igbo society and I cannot be "repaired" when lunatics like the angry and mis-educated Briton at Novotel Hotel are allowed to *imagine* 'others' unchecked by society and government.

My friend, Horowitz, in his characteristic critique of my ideas as "You're asking the government to police the imagination?"

Yes, it is the responsibility of the government to identify and isolate mentally retarded citizens because I am convinced that the British man had a psychiatric problem.

On another occasion, my colleague, an African American professor had asked me, "Ewa, how do you designate yourself in application forms? Do you call yourself an African American, or Black, or what else?" She quickly added, "I hope you don't ever call yourself an African American, because that name describes our ancestors who were brought into slavery and who helped to build America's wealth and institutions. Your ancestors don't have that history, so you are not entitled to the benefits of our historical labor and our agony. You came to America by air while our ancestors came by sea."

I responded, "The African American designation is all yours, Professor." Even the Black people suffer from the imaginative karma. Could it make any difference, if I disclosed to my cynical colleague that I am married to a Liberian woman who is a relative of the legendary Harriet Tubman. My friend might never have heard about President WVS Tubman of Liberia or the historic relationship between Liberia and the United States. So while I'm completely entangled in blood and spirit with my African American relatives, some of them are not aware of the Kamenu or common karma which ties us together.

15

OLAUDA'S TIMELINE

Onye Macharu Iwhe Uwa – Who knows and who understands this world?

I have come to realize that the agony of the Africanworld has no comparison anywhere else. Recent times have brought emotional arguments about apology and reparative justice for slavery. Yet the question of how oppressed and traumatized people should deal with their past is a difficult one. Toward reconciliation and national recovery in the 21ˢᵗ century, any society that ignores the historical wrongdoings and human rights violations of the past is likely more vulnerable to a tumultuous future and insecurity. When politicians begin to evoke the memories of slavery, they are not only exhuming the unhealed past but also the experiences *of* Olauda, the ordinary Igbo teenager with an extraordinary story and the millions of other slaves whom his *interesting narrative* represents.

As usual, my friend Horowitz, questions my sense of judgement, "Your point is that African suffering is much worse than any other suffering? How do you reach this conclusion?"

Ewa: Which other ethnic people worldwide suffered the commodification of it's people like the Africans? Take the case of Olauda:

Olauda Ikwueno, an eleven-year-old Igbo boy, was kidnapped with his sister and sold into slavery. Separately, they experienced the agony and torture of the trans-Atlantic slave trade. He was shipped to Barbados, to Britain, and to the United States by British slave traders. Ironically, it was Aro people, members of a sub-group from the same Igbo ethnic nation, who kidnapped them. Igbos were, therefore, complicit in the violation of the dignity and humanity of their own children.

1745   Olauda Ikwueno is born in what is now Nigeria.

1756   Slavers kidnap him and his sister.

1766   Olauda earns enough money to buy his own freedom.

1773   Olauda joins an expedition to find the Northwest Passage.

1775   Olauda travels to Central America to set up a new type of plantation.

1786   Olauda becomes part of the Sierra Leone resettlement project.

1787   The Society for the Abolition of the Slave trade is founded in Britain.

1789   The French Revolution begins. Its idea of liberty for all encourages rebellion in the slave colonies.

1789   Olauda publishes his autobiography. It becomes a bestseller.

1792   Olauda marries Susanna Cullen.

1797   Olauda dies.

1807   The British Parliament passes the law for the abolition of the slave trade across the Atlantic Ocean.

1833   Slavery is abolished in the British colonies.

1865   Slavery is abolished in the United States at the end of the American Civil War.[17]

---

17   Thomas, Paul, and Victor Ambrus. "A Timeline." Olauda Ikwuenu: From Slavery to Freedom, 1st ed., Printing Express Limited, Hong Kong, 2007, pp. 46–47.

16

THE TRIANGULAR TRADE

Ije eluwa – The Journey of life.

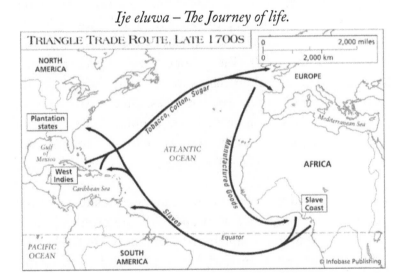

From West Africa to Europe and to the Americas.

The Trans-Atlantic Slave Trade had three stages:[18]

STAGE 1

Slave ships from Britain left ports like London, Liverpool and Bristol for West Africa carrying goods such as cloth, guns, ironware and drink that had been made in Britain.

STAGE 2

African slave dealers kidnapped people from villages up to hundreds of miles inland. One of these people was Quobna Ottabah Cugoano, born in Ghana some twelve years after Olauda, who described in his autobiography how slavers attacked with pistols and threatened to kill those who did not obey. They marched the captives to the coast where they were traded for goods. The prisoners were forced to march long distances with their hands tied behind their backs and their necks connected by wooden yokes. On the African coast, European traders bought enslaved peoples from travelling African dealers or nearby African chiefs. Families were separated.

The traders held the enslaved Africans until a ship appeared, and then sold them to a European or African captain. It often took a long time for a captain to fill his ship. He rarely filled his ship in one spot. Instead, he would spend three to four months sailing along the coast, looking for the fittest and cheapest slaves.

Ships would sail up and down the coast filling their holds with enslaved Africans. On the brutal Middle Passage, enslaved

18   https://commons.wikimedia.org/wiki/File:Slave_route.jpg.

Africans were densely packed onto ships that would carry them to the West Indies.

There were many cases of violent resistance by Africans against slave ships and their crews. These included attacks from the shore by free Africans against ships or longboats and many cases of shipboard revolt by slaves.

STAGE 3

In the West Indies, enslaved Africans would be sold to the highest bidder at slave auctions. Once they had been bought, they worked for nothing on plantations.

They belonged to the plantation owner, like any other possession, and had no rights at all. The enslaved Africans were often punished very harshly.

Enslaved Africans resisted their enslavement in many ways, from violent revolution to silent, personal resistance. Some refused to be enslaved and took their own lives. Sometimes pregnant women preferred abortion to bringing a child into slavery.

On the plantations, many enslaved Africans tried to slow down the pace of work by pretending to be ill, setting fires, or "accidentally" breaking tools. Whenever possible, they ran away. Some escaped to South America, England, or North America. There were hundreds of slave revolts.

Two-thirds of the enslaved Africans taken to the Americas ended up on sugar plantations. Sugar was used to sweeten another crop harvested by enslaved Africans in the West Indies: coffee.

With the money made from the sale of enslaved Africans, goods such as sugar, coffee and tobacco were bought and carried back to Britain for sale. The ships were loaded with produce from the plantations for the voyage home.[19]

19   *The Abolition Project.* East of England Broadband Network, abolition.e2bn.org/ slavery_43.html. Accessed 14 Nov. 2019.

17

CARICOM

Onye ma Uchem? – Who can read my mind?
According to the slave narratives, most of the enslaved Igbo people
were shipped to the Caribbean, especially to Bahamas, Barbados,
Cuba, Haiti, and Jamaica. Compensation to the descendants of the
enslaved Africans in the diaspora has become a global campaign.

In 2013, Caribbean Heads of Government established the Caricom Reparations Commission (CRC) with a mandate to prepare the case for reparatory justice for the region's indigenous and African descendant communities who are the victims of Crimes against Humanity (CAH) in the forms of genocide, slavery, slave trading, and racial apartheid.

This document, prepared by the CRC, proposes the delivery of this mandate within the formulation of the Caricom Reparations Justice Program (CRJP). The CRC asserts that victims and descendants of these CAH have a legal right to reparatory justice, and that those who committed these crimes, and who have been enriched by the proceeds of these crimes, have a reparatory case to answer.

The CRC Asserts That European Governments:

- Were owners and traders of enslaved Africans instructed genocidal actions upon indigenous communities
- Created the legal, financial, and fiscal policies necessary for the enslavement of Africans
- Defined and enforced African enslavement and native genocide as in their 'national interests'
- Refused compensation to the enslaved with the ending of their enslavement
- Compensated slave owners at emancipation for the loss of legal property rights in enslaved Africans
- Imposed a further one hundred years of racial apartheid upon the emancipated
- Imposed for another one hundred years policies designed to perpetuate suffering upon the emancipated and survivors of genocide
- And have refused to acknowledge such crimes or to compensate victims and their descendants

TEN POINT ACTION PLAN

- Full Formal Apology
- Repatriation
- Indigenous Peoples Development Program
- Cultural Institutions
- Public Health Crisis
- Illiteracy Eradication
- African Knowledge Program
- Psychological Rehabilitation
- Technology Transfer

- 10. Debt Cancellation[20]

20   20. https://caricomreparations.org/caricom/caricoms-10-point-reparation-plan.

18

LETTER FROM PATTERSON

Osondi Owendi – What makes some people happy, makes others sad.

Patterson's Open Letter to Cameron

On Tuesday, September 30, 2015, the Prime Minister of Britain, David Cameron, addressed Jamaica's parliament.

Jamaica's former Prime Minister, P.J. Patterson, responded. Excerpts from his response: 'Verbatim;'

"Prime Minister, the most noble intentions were jarred by those portions of your address which asserted that slavery was a long time ago, in the historical past, and as friends we can move on together to build for the future.[21]"

Your host, The Most Hon. Portia Simpson-Miller, in her gracious welcome referred to the difficult issue of reparation which should be discussed in "a spirit of mutual respect, openness and understanding as we seek to actively engage the U.K. on the matter."

You chose instead to throw down the gauntlet.

Mere acknowledgement of its horror will not suffice.

It was and still is a most heinous crime against humanity — a stain which cannot be removed merely by the passage of time.

The attempt to trivialize and diminish the significance of 300 years of British enslavement of Africans and the trade in their bodies reflect the continued ethnic targeting of our ancestors and their progeny for discriminatory treatment in both the annals of history and in the present.

The 180 years of slavery in Jamaica remain fresh in living memory. There are people alive in Jamaica today whose great-grandparents were a part of the slavery system and the memory of slavery still lingers in these households and communities.

21

Those 180 years were followed by another 100 years of imposed racial apartheid in which these families were racially oppressed by British armies and colonial machinery. The scars of this oppression are still alive in the minds and hearts of million Jamaicans.

To speak of slavery as something from the Middle Ages is insufficient. For our communities, its legacies are still present in their memory and emotions. To reject this living experience is to repudiate the very meaning and existence of these people's lives. How can we simply forget it and move on to the future? If there is no explicit admission of guilt now, when will be the proper time?

You argue that Britain abolished the slave system and the credit for this resonates in the British Parliament today and shows British compassion and diplomacy.

Where is the prior confession that Britain fashioned, legalized, perpetuated, and prospered from the slave trade?

Indeed, the facts speak to a different explanation. In Jamaica, the enslaved led by Sam Sharpe tried to abolish slavery themselves three years before your Parliament acted. The British army destroyed these freedom fighters and executed their leaders.

This attempt to destroy the seed of freedom and justice in Jamaica continued for another hundred years. In 1865 the peasants sought to occupy Crown lands in order to survive widespread hunger. The British government sent in the army and massacred those people, executing Paul Bogle, George William Gordon, and other Leaders.

Furthermore, the British Act of Emancipation reflected that the enslaved people of Jamaica were not human but property. The 800,000 Africans in the Caribbean and elsewhere were valued at £47 million. The government agreed to compensate the slave owners £20 million and passed an Emancipation Act in which the enslaved had to work free for another four to six years in order to work off the £27 million promised slave owners. It was they who paid for their eventual freedom.

The enslaved paid more than 50 per cent of the cost of their market value in compensation to slave owners. This is what your Emancipation Act did. The enslaved got nothing by way of compensation. The Act of Emancipation was self-serving and was designed to support British national commercial interests alone.

You have refused to apologise. Yet your government has apologised to everyone else for horrid crimes. Are we not worthy of an apology or less deserving?

Mere acknowledgement of the crime is insufficient. The international community and international law call for formal apologies when crimes against humanity are committed. The UN has deemed slave trading and slavery as crimes against humanity. The refusal to apologise is a refusal to take responsibility for the crime. In a law-abiding world, this is not acceptable.

Contrary to your view, the Caribbean people will never emerge completely from the "long, dark shadow" of slavery until there is a full confession of guilt by those who committed this evil atrocity.

"The resilience and spirit of its people" is no ground to impair the solemnity of a privileged Parliamentary occasion and allow the memory of our ancestors to be offended once again.

The Caribbean people have long been looking to the future. This is what we do in our development visions, but these legacies are like millstones around our necks. We look to reparatory justice as the beginning of shaping a new future. We invite Britain to engage in removing this blot on human civilisation so that together we can create a new and secure future.[22]

ONE LOVE.
Yours sincerely,
P.J. Patterson
Former Prime Minister, Jamaica (1992-2006)

Having reproduced Patterson's epic letter on reparation, how do governments, societies, and victims deal with the *injustices* of the past? Should perpetrator-countries be pardoned or punished? If so, how? These questions become especially important for societies making the transition from dictatorship to democracy: Germany after Nazism, South Africa after Apartheid, Democratization in Latin America, Democratization in Eastern Europe, and reparation to the post-slavery societies, which is our primary concern in this book.

Reparative justice in our present day is a controversial theme. The concept of morality continues to weaken among states and religious authorities as Trumpism and American televangelists indicate in these *uncertain* times. In an internet and virtual

---

22   RJRGLEANER Communications Group. "Former Prime Minister PJ Patterson Has Penned an Open Letter to British Prime Minister David Cameron Telling Him That Jamaica Deserves an Apology from Britain for Slavery." The Gleaner [Kingston, Jamaica], 8 Oct. 2015, jamaica-gleaner.com/article/news/20151008/full-text-pj-slams-david-cameron-are-we-not-worthy-he-asks.

age, which witnesses the erosion of moral values, many people wonder if there still exists any acceptable moral code to guide humanity. My friend Nat counters my argument and insists that more people than ever are "throwing themselves into some kind of religion." Sometimes, we might wish to observe certain spiritual laws in order to discover the truth about the Karma around our neck and the invisible prison we are caged in.

On the topic of reparation, the late *Eckankar High Initiate* and spiritual teacher, Humphrey Amaechina wrote, "Briefly, my view is that we Africans should first apologise to ourselves before asking the white man to pay us for that tragic experience."

Karma or Kamenu – is a universal law that holds all life together. The trans-Atlantic slave trade was an ancestral karma and not a punishment from God. The human family has a complex and inseparable Karma since we are, indeed, our own ancestors.

According to oral narratives, during the *Golden Age* of Africa, the ancient peoples of Europe and the Americas were enslaved and humiliated by the West Africans of that period. This is the missing link in the past and present debates on reparation.

Horowitz: "By the term *ancestral Karma*, do you mean that the people who were kidnapped were receiving the necessary expiatory punishment for what their ancestors had done?

Ewa: Most likely so. Kamenuists believe that every guilt, collective or individual must be atoned by sacrifice. The guilt incurred is not *sin* but an act of commission or omission by our ancestors could affect us because in reality we are our own ancestors. Recall that Olauda's father kept some slaves himself. In his narrative his son, Olauda had the premonition or strong feeling that one day he would be kidnapped. The point I want to make is not that it's impossible for the punishment to fit the crime, but that only the law of karma itself can create a payback which ought not be seen as punishment but as a balancing action and reaction. In other words, justice for slavery comes not from humans but from the universe itself.

Horowitz: "So was Patterson wrong to be annoyed with Cameron? Because saying that justice is divine or natural or whatever still leaves unanswered the question of what we humans should do in order to move forward."

Ewa: The secret to a deeper and happier life is to develop your spiritual *Self*. Patterson is neither wrong nor right to get angry with Cameron. It depends on their levels of spiritual consciousness and their societies too. Resolution or payment of reparation will occur when each society has burnt or dissolved or wiped out the past Karma that brought their current citizens back into this physical universe.

Kamenu can simply be described as the law of karma, the law of compensation, the law of give and take, the law of cause and effect. They all mean the same thing. Ultimately, the law of Karma is inescapable: we must reap what we sow in this life and in our past life.

19

THIS IS NOT HOW LIFE WORKS

Osuoffia – The forest clearer – Bulldozer.

The spiritual law of karma is not like our national law. We cannot possibly outsmart, bypass or manipulate the law of Kamenu. Some people choose to ignore it, while others argue, "This is not how life works." The latter group believes there is no justice in this world, therefore, there is no need to think of wrong and right in this world.

Horowitz disagrees, this looks like a straw man argument. Germany killed millions of people, including 6 million Jews. Today, Germany is the biggest economy in Europe. No ancestral curses there.

Ewa: That's the point. Inweronye scholars recollect that in September 1952, Germany paid Israel a whooping expiatory sum of 3 billion marks over the next fourteen years. Subsequently, 450 million marks was paid to the World Jewish Congress. This reparation payment between Germany and Israel atoned for the German Holocaust and created the spiritual harmony for reconciliation, economic abundance and catharsis.

Horowitz: In Africa, every day, pastors are telling us about ancestral curses. What actually did our ancestors do?"[23] Despite our limited knowledge of the causal roots of what we term injustices, still the forces of action and reaction do control us. If we choose to become more sensitive to understanding the law of Kamenu, then it could likely help us in understanding the spiritual causes and effects of what we simply regard as past injustices such as the slavery issue.

Ewa: My American pal, Horowitz, thinks "this is a faith-based, and rather weak, argument: "we don't understand Kamenu, but if we choose to become more sensitive to it, it could likely help us."

My response is ironically in harmony. "In Africa, every day, pastors are telling us about ancestral curses." When the Europeans invaded Africa, they came with their 3 Cs to:

Colonize

Civilize and

Christianize

African people. Before the British left after independence, missionaries had etched it on African minds that our reward is in Heaven and not in this world; that only the poor shall inherit the Kingdom of God; that if someone slaps you, you should turn the other cheek. Finally, in my Igbo ethnic

---

23 Anonymous Twitter user

nation, they scolded us for bearing the Igbo names our parents named us. In place of our given names, they forced us to adopt Catholic names of dead Italian Saints. Hence today, there is hardly any other society so humiliated and so exploited and abused. When it was time for me to be baptized, Ogbunku the Catechist, asked me to pick an Italian Saint's name. He explained that my name Ewa was satanic and that I could not enter the Kingdom of God with my satanic indigenous name. The post-independence period soon plunged us into series of military dictatorship, Civil War, poverty and hopelessness. During the War, Igbo fought and prayed but prayers gave way to might. In the United States, if you are sick you go to see a physician while Nigerians are dying in droves for curable diseases. In Nigeria, if you are sick you pray and go to your priest or pastor. If you have marriage issues you avoid trained counselors and head to your priest – a bachelor man who has taken the celibacy oath and who has no experience about marriage issues.

Finally, Horowitz writes "We don't understand Kamenu, but if we choose to become more sensitive to it, it could likely help us." Most of my fellow Euro-American scholars ought to know that in the new post-Trump and post-COVID19 world, we now live in the transitional state of change in academic freedom and diversity curricula. The new Inweronye Awakening will reject trite Eurocentric theories that insist that every conceivable idea originated from Europe or from the West. Inweronye and Kamenu belong to the emergent New Order.

My friend Horwitz, in the new awakening which gives voice to the long-muted minority viewpoint, *faith-based* arguments are rather NOT weak arguments. "We don't understand Kamenu, but if we choose to become more sensitive to it, it could likely help us." The choice is yours. Diversity in theory is an idea whose time has come.

20

YOUNG AFRICAN AMERICAN VOICES

Ome Ife Ukwu – The leader who does great things.

"African Americans should be paid reparation because slavery is something that a human being should never go through. If slavery never happened, most African Americans would be in Africa. Our ancestors were robbed of their history." – Ahshantie[24]

"That was their time. Now is our time. They had their time but they chose to do all those wrongs. We shouldn't be held responsible for their actions." – *Vanessa*

"I highly disagree with this idea of paying reparation for the slavery injustices. This is an unusual scenario. It is 2019, we are ALL equal, and there should be no compensation for things that went on decades ago… It just doesn't make sense to me!

---

24   Ahshantie

It is too confusing and there would be no way to go through the process accurately... Plus, we have so much going on in the world at this time, we should all be focusing on the present, not worrying about the past. The past is the PAST." – *Cornish*

"Americans *should pay reparations* for the injustices of slavery. It is necessary to acknowledge our wrongdoings because this country failed slaves and put them through awful circumstances. Just like we should have immense amounts of sympathy for the Native Americans, because like slaves, this country put them through awful circumstances. America has tried to help Native Americans with lower tuition rates, they have their own reservations where some don't have to pay state income taxes, and they have provided some money and reservations for housing units." – *Anonymous*

"America should pay reparations to their victims just like Germany did to their Jewish victims. In fact, America actually helped the Jewish victims in receiving their reparations from Germany. The United States have paid reparations in the past for their wrongdoings, but they haven't paid to victims of slavery.

Reparations are not only financial aids, it also forces the United States to admit they did something wrong to their people. Unfortunately, the U.S. has a long way to go... because so many people are against providing financial aid or acknowledging how awful slavery truly was. I think it is an extremely complicated process, but it would be right thing to do for the victims of slavery." – *Riley*[25]

As we have seen, there are clashing views between the African American and the African perspectives on the question of

---

25   Riley

reparation to enslaved descendants. My buddy contends, "No, we haven't seen the African perspective on this topic." Yes, the African perspective has been clearly stated, The Africans believe in Kamenuic justice, which the Orientals call Karma. Africans believe that monetary reparation cannot absolve slave perpetrators from blood guilt.

Horowitz opines that the universe has a way of working these things out. You haven't said directly whether you favor monetary compensation or not. And is your perspective "the African perspective"? Finally, you haven't told us clearly, either, what you think is "the African-American perspective."

Ewa: In transitional justice theory and practice, my duty as a storyteller is to present the facts as I know it without taking sides. I favor neither monetary nor spiritual reparation, yet I am not against any of the methods. I do not therefore represent the African perspective but the world view or my own homeland Ezza. For fear of repeating myself, I want to emphatically tell my friend that while the African American perspective favors reparation, the African continent's view is not necessarily monetary compensation, but rather a spiritual world view which relies on the idea of cause and effect. This does not mean that Africans will not accept monetary reparation if a benevolent society offers one.

So far none of the contending views of Horowitz speaks to the spiritual side of the slavery issue. Humphrey's last letter will shine more light on the spiritual argument.[26]

---

26   The views expressed are those of students at Wyandotte High School.

21

THE DANGER OF IMAGINING 'OTHERS'.

Ogbuefi Nna Nyelu Ugo – The title holder whom God has blessed.

R ecall that on May 14, 2000, Humphrey Amaechina wrote me from his home in New Jersey what becomes his last letter. Recall also that Amaechina was a Higher Initiate of Eckankar – the Religion of the Light and Sound of God.

Recall that in the letter, he says, "What you can do, but not when you are studying [doctoral studies at Howard university] is to write a good book on REPARATION TO AFRICA." In his final words he further writes, "We Africans should first apologize to ourselves before asking the white man to pay us for that tragic experience [because] the law of karma is strong."

On September 1, 2002, Humphrey *translated* (died) at the prime age of 62 years. The Eckists believe that people translate. People do not die. Rather, they change form. The soul does not die. What Humphrey wants us to know is that the law of karma is very strong when we reckon with the injustices of the past, especially, on the issue of slavery and reparation. Ezza people insist, whether we believe it or not, that karma is real.

At the end of my doctoral studies at Howard University, also Humphrey's alma mater, I turned my attention to the Higher Initiate's assignment, only to discover that past debates on reparation had been unimaginably flawed in many ways. First, nothing new has emerged from such past debates. Second, there had been intense focus on financial compensation only to African Americans. Compensation to African Americans only, though well-meaning, is a one-sided prescription that ignores the African side of the crime and story. Third, while most of the victims of the trans-Atlantic slavery came from West Africa, especially the Igbo ethnic nation, as recorded in Olauda's *Interesting Narrative,* the latter had been constantly excluded from the reparation debate. Fourth, the debate, so far, has not dealt with the spiritual healing aspect of the slave question and reparation.

Ewa: On the argument "that nothing new has emerged from such paste debates,"

Horowitz disagrees:

Now, I think I see that you may be arguing that Igbos deserve compensation for slavery too. But you're not stating it directly, nor do you justify the point. Compensation for Igbos including Aros? Excluding Aros? Compensation for all Africans, whether their ancestors or relatives were involved or not?

My response is simple. In a transitional justice discourse as this one, the storyteller must present both sides of the argument without taking sides. In this case, I have chosen to remain neutral. However, I am now compelled to answer your questions. Yes, Igbos deserve compensation for the past unpaid labor of their relatives during slavery, but that is after apologizing to the African Americans and African diaspora for the wrongdoings of the Aros and other enablers. Truth and Reconciliation Commissions (TRC) should be established to document the Aros and other perpetrators in order to punish and deter or forgive and forget the past. Although slavery is a universal phenomenon, however, the trans-Atlantic slave trade will be limited to West Africa.

Therefore, compensation for all Africans, whether their ancestors or relatives were involved or not is a wrong idea. In an earlier presentation at Goldsmith University of London in August 2019, I had warned that post-slavery societies, while seeking their human rights to justice, must be careful not to create new zones of injustices by demanding reparation from white societies in the 21st century.

It is wrong to ask me to pay for the past injustices my late parents committed. The past debates are flawed because nothing new has come of them. Then what is the substance that is old in them? You can't criticize all past debates because they are not new. Of course, they are not new. "Take away this expensive bottle of wine! It is not new!"

"Nothing new" as used here is a metaphorical way of saying that past debates on reparation failed to bring reconciliation, healing and national recovery. The recent rightwing mob insurrection on March 6, 2021 at the Capitol in Washington D.C. is a wake-up call that black and white rage are on the increase in America.

I contend, therefore that what the post-Atlantic slavery societies need most is not financial compensation. Some societies need spiritual reparation, some need transitional justice reparation such as the establishment of truth commissions that would allow the descendants of enslaved people to tell their stories. When governments make just decisions, then societies will reconcile and heal towards national recovery. In a post-Black-Lives-Matter, post-Trumpism and post-Insurrectionist society, what matters most now is national healing and reconciliation.

For Ndigbo (Igbo people) no amount of compensation can *right* the *wrongs* meted to Olauda and the muted voices of those whose stories and experiences died in captivity.[27]

Horowitz: "Are you arguing against financial compensation, or arguing that something else is needed as well? Your words are ambiguous.

Ewa: "My argument is that individuals, families, nations and societies are not on the same level of spiritual consciousness and as such, cannot be treated alike. When it comes to reparation, it is not one size fits all approach. Like Humphrey, I would think that the African people should apologize to Black diaspora for past acts of commission and omission of their ancestors before seeking any form of financial reparation.

Karma and Olauda

We recall that one victim of the evil of slavery described above is Olauda Ikwueno (1745-1797), who was also known as Gustavus Vassa, an Igbo posthumously adopted as a son of Unwu Adakaogu, Ntsokara, Ezza in Ebonyi State, Nigeria.

---

27 Humphrey Amaechina's last letter to Ewa Unoke, dated 05/14/2000.

Horowitz contends, "Again, there's absolutely no reason for us to believe this assertion."

My pal Horowitz is making a legitimate claim according to the research ethics of a typical American graduate school rules and regulations. However, from an African lens, I had exhumed Olauda's story and "body" from London in 2019 for a dignified burial and celebration of his life as an Ezza prince. From freedom to captivity and as the author of the first written history of the Igbo nation in his legendary book, "The Interesting Narratives of Olaudah Equiano…" Ntsokara and Ezza and myself have adopted Olauda as our son.

Olauda's story is more than a tale about bondage and justice, though slavery was an important part of his life. It is the story of one Igbo man who encountered this brutal world and learned how to survive in it, physically and spiritually. In telling the story of one who survived, Ikwueno tells the stories of countless others who did not.[28]

According to the narrative, slavery was not new to Olauda, because his father owned slaves. Since the elder Ikwueno owned slaves, and his own son and daughter were kidnapped and sold into slavery, this is indeed Kamenu or the law of karma at work. You reap what you sow. Olauda, in his narratives alluded to his "fate" many times. In Igboland and among other African people, men and women became slaves through warfare and not by being traded like inanimate objects. Sometimes people were enslaved as punishment for committing such crimes as theft or adultery. In his *interesting narrative*, Olauda laments

---

28   The Life of Olaudah Equiano. 1st ed., vol. 1, DOVER PUBLICATIONS, INC., 1999. Book
      Preface. p. vii

that slavery had not only deprived him of freedom but had cut him off from the Igbo spiritual universe. ibid. p.5[29]

In his book, Olauda found comfort in the stories of the ancient Jews, whose customs, creation legends and social structures reminded him of his "Ibo world." But on October 6, 1774, Olauda, the kidnapped victim whose book influenced the British government to abolish slavery became a free man.

In the world of antislavery, Olauda's parallel themes of freedom and salvation had also become the central themes of the antislavery movement in England. The US presidential candidates who were engaged in the slave debate ought to be able to stop imagining in order to understand the slave experience and narrative especially as told by victims themselves.

Africa and Europe had imagined Olauda as a non-person. His new owners shackled his hands and feet. Olauda's limbs are the limbs of nobody. The African slave had become the bastard-child of humanity. Most times, our opinions about slave reparation are shaped by the way we imagine the victims either as people or as property. For too long, the advocates of the imaginative solution had by-passed constitutional solution. The biggest looming question in the United States today concerning the politics of apology and reparation involves the legacy of trans-Atlantic slavery. Union General, William Tecumseh Sherman's post-Civil War promise of "forty acres and a mule" for freed slaves never came to be.

---

29   The life of Olaudah Equiano p.7.

22

40 ACRES AND A MULE

Oka Ome – Promises fulfilled or unfulfilled.

In Henry Louis Gates' Words

We've all heard the story of the "40 acres and a mule" promise to former slaves. It's a staple of black history lessons, and it's the name of Spike Lee's film company. The promise was the first systematic attempt to provide a form of reparations to newly freed slaves, and it was astonishingly radical for its time, proto-socialist in its implications. In fact, such a policy would be radical in any country today: the federal government's massive confiscation of private property — some 400,000 acres — formerly owned by Confederate landowners, and its methodical redistribution to former black slaves. What most of us haven't heard is that the idea really was generated by black leaders themselves.

It is difficult to stress adequately how revolutionary this idea was: As the historian Eric Foner puts it in his book,

Reconstruction: America's Unfinished Revolution, 1863-1877, "Here in coastal South Carolina and Georgia, the prospect beckoned of a transformation of Southern society more radical even than the end of slavery." Try to imagine how profoundly different the history of race relations in the United States would have been had this policy been implemented and enforced; had the former slaves actually had access to the ownership of land, of property; if they had had a chance to be self-sufficient economically, to build, accrue and pass on wealth. After all, one of the principal promises of America was the possibility of average people being able to own land, and all that such ownership entailed. As we know all too well, this promise was not to be realized for most of the nation's former slaves, which numbered about 3.9 million.

While monetary compensation might be acceptable to African Americans, it is not likely that Olauda's homeland - Ezza would accept blood money as legitimate expiation for the karma associated with the infamous trans-Atlantic slave trade. Ezza Kamenuists, like the Puritans and the Quakers believe that the freedom and dignity diminished or destroyed by slavery must be repaired or restored. Restorative justice could be done voluntarily, or perpetrators must accept the unstoppable retributive punishment from the law of Kamenu also known as Karma. As a Kamenuist, I suggest, therefore, that while Eurocentric reparation seeks economic remedy in this physical universe, the Ezza-Igbo-centric restorative justice is more concerned with spiritual atonement. The repercussions from slavery which plague our societies today, cannot be repaired with economic justice alone, but must be combined with spiritual cleansing, healing and catharsis.

Horowitz: So, you approve of monetary reparations?

Ewa: I am not in a position to say yes or no. As a Kamenuist, I have the right to consciously disentangle my physical and astral bodies from the Ezza (Igbo) collective Karma. Money cannot wipe away blood guilt. It is therefore left for every individual, family, nation and society to evaluate their level of spiritual or moral consciousness to determine when they are ready to tell the truth, to seek justice and to reconcile.

Horowitz: Are there Igbos currently clamoring for expiation? Would the Igbos seriously turn down an offer of a large sum of cash from Europe or the USA intended to apologize for abusing people in the past?

Ewa: The Igbo people have a saying that God comes first in their lives. But after God comes money. This explains the *Igbo achievement* mantra – Igbo nagba mbo (Igbos work hard to succeed). Currently there are freedom and reparation movements arising in Igboland. Yes, there is an *Igbo Awakening*. Igbos would not turn down boxes of pounds and dollar notes from Europe and America because in reality both societies have not balanced their spiritual and economic accounts.

However, Ndigbo need to be reminded to do a continental and global spiritual cleansing and apology before accepting any form of reparation which indeed is regarded as blood money by Ezza Kamenuists.

Are we, now, determined to save succeeding generations from the karma of slavery which has continued to bring untold agony and sorrow to humanity? Can we reaffirm faith in the fundamental human rights and dignity of men, women, and children?

23

BLACK ANGER

Eze Udo – The peace maker.

The reparative justice question is an unfinished business, activists argue, because African Americans are still angry, and such black anger manifests itself in various segments of the society. I will argue that the African American society has not fully recovered from the effects of slavery, or from the tumultuous events of 1968, either.

1968 was one of the most chaotic years of the 20th century in the United States. On April 4, 1968, Martin Luther King Jr., an American Christian minister and activist who became the most visible spokesperson and leader in the Civil Rights Movement, was assassinated. On the evening of Thursday, April 4, as word of King's assassination in Memphis, Tennessee spread, crowds began to gather at the intersection of 14th and U Streets in Washington D.C. Stokely Carmichael, the militant civil and political rights activist who had parted with King in 1966 and had been removed as head of the Student Nonviolent

Coordinating Committee in 1967, led members of the SNCC to stores in the neighborhood demanding that they close out of respect. Although polite at first, the crowd fell out of control and began breaking windows. Carmichael, who supported the riots, told rioters to "go home and get your guns."[30]

The disturbances began when a window was broken at the People's Drug Store at the intersection of 14th and U Streets, NW. An hour and half later, by 11 p.m., window-smashing and looting spread throughout the area. Looting occurred generally where there was little police protection. The local police department could not handle the disturbance. As one officer said, "This situation is out of control, and we need help, it's too much for us to handle." The civil disturbance unit was later activated, but by the time order was restored around 3 a.m., 200 stores had their windows broken and 150 stores were looted, most of them emptied. Liquor stores were hardest hit. Black store owners wrote "Soul Brother" on their storefronts so that rioters would spare their stores.

The D.C. fire department reported 1,180 fires between March 30 and April 14 of 1968 as arsonists set buildings ablaze.

On June 5, 1968, the African American community was further provoked when presidential candidate Robert F. Kennedy was mortally wounded shortly after midnight at the Ambassador Hotel in Los Angeles. Earlier that evening, the 42-year-old junior senator from New York was declared the winner in the South Dakota and California presidential primaries in the 1968 election. He was pronounced dead at 1:44 a.m. on June 6, about 26 hours after he had been shot.[30]

---

30   The Life of Olaudah Equiano p.5.

Following dual victories in the California and South Dakota primary elections for the Democratic nomination for President of the United States, Senator Kennedy spoke to journalists and campaign workers at a live televised celebration from the stage of his headquarters at the Ambassador Hotel. Shortly after leaving the podium and exiting through a kitchen hallway, he was mortally wounded by multiple shots fired from a handgun. Kennedy died in the Good Samaritan Hospital 26 hours later. The shooter was a 24-year-old Sirhan Sirhan. In 1969, Sirhan was convicted of murdering the senator and sentenced to death. His sentence was commuted to life in prison in 1972. A freelance newspaper reporter recorded the shooting on audio tape, and the aftermath was captured on film.

1968: A Significant Year

- February 1 – Two Memphis sanitation workers are killed in the line of duty, exacerbating labor tensions.
- February 8 – The Orangeburg Massacre occurs during university protest in South Carolina.
- February 12 – First day of the (wildcat) Memphis Sanitation Strike
- March – While filming a prime time television special, Petula Clark touches Harry Belafonte's arm during a duet. Chrysler Corporation, the show's sponsor, insists the moment be deleted, but Clark stands firm, destroys all other takes of the song, and delivers the completed program to NBC with the touch intact. The show is broadcast on April 8, 1968.[64]
- April 3 – King returns to Memphis; delivers "Mountaintop" speech.
- April 4 – Dr. King is shot and killed in Memphis,

Tennessee.

- April 4–8 and one on May 1968 – Riots break out in Chicago, Washington, D.C., Baltimore, Louisville, Kansas City, and more than 150 U.S. cities in response to the assassination of Dr. King.
- April 11 – Civil Rights Act of 1968 is signed. The Fair Housing Act is Title VIII of this Civil Rights Act – it bans discrimination in the sale, rental, and financing of housing. The law is passed following a series of contentious open housing campaigns throughout the urban North. The most significant of these campaigns was the Chicago Open Housing Movement of 1966 and organized events in Milwaukee during 1967–68. In both cities, angry white mobs attacked nonviolent protesters.
- May 12 – Poor People's Campaign marches on Washington, DC.
- June 6 – Senator Robert F. Kennedy, a Civil Rights advocate, is assassinated after winning the California presidential primary. His appeal to minorities helped him secure the victory.
- September 17 – Diahann Carroll stars in the title role in *Julia*, as the first African-American actress to star in her own television series where she did not play a domestic worker.
- October 3 – The play *The Great White Hope* opens; it runs for 546 performances and later becomes a film.
- October – Tommie Smith and John Carlos raise their fists to symbolize black power and unity after winning the gold and bronze medals, respectively, at the 1968 Summer Olympic Games.
- November 22 – First interracial kiss on American

television, between Michelle Nichols and William Shatner on *Star Trek*.

- In *Powe v. Miles*, a federal court holds that the portions of private colleges that are funded by public money are subject to the Civil Rights Act.
- Shirley Chisholm becomes the first African American woman elected to Congress.

Police Brutality

About 1 in 1,000 black men and boys in America can expect to die at the hands of police, according to a new analysis of deaths involving law enforcement officers. That makes them 2.5 times more likely than white men and boys to die during an encounter with cops.

The analysis also showed that Latino men and boys, black women and girls and Native American men, women and children are also killed by police at higher rates than their white peers. But the vulnerability of black males was particularly striking.

"That 1-in-1,000 number struck us as quite high," said study leader Frank Edwards, a sociologist at Rutgers University. "That's better odds of being killed by police than you have of winning a lot of scratch-off lottery games."

The number-crunching by Edwards and his coauthors also revealed that for all young men, police violence was one of the leading causes of death in the years 2013 to 2018.

Deadly Toll of Police Violence

A new study finds that about 1 in 1,000 black men and boys can expect to die because of police violence over the course of their lives – a risk that's about 2.5 times higher than their white peers. The annual risk rises and falls with age and is highest for young men. Here is how it compares to other leading causes of death for black men in their mid-to-late 20s.

Cause of death	Mortality rate
Assault	94.2
Accidents	52.1
Suicide	17.5
Heart disease	14
HIV	6.8
Cancer	6.2
Police use of force*	3.4
Diabetes	2.8
Influenza and pneumonia	2
Chronic lower respiratory disease	2
Cerebrovascular diseases	1.9

Annual mortality rates are reported as deaths per 100,000 black men ages 25 to 29.

The conclusion that we arrive from the above study shows that the black communities in America are an endangered species of humanity, quite vulnerable to police brutality and death. In other words, the culture of violence and hate today in our societies are all attributable to the scourge of slavery.

The misinterpretations of African American society and African society began with half-lies and half-truths told by early missionaries and European theorists, especially the German philosopher Georg Wilhelm Friedrich Hegel.

24

THE DIFFICULTY OF IMAGINING OTHERS

Ochili Ozua – King of Diversity who believes in the people's general welfare.

Hegel and Trevor-Roper: The Difficulty of Imagining Others

It is an irony that we should start the study of the African world and slavery with a German philosopher's theory. In his work, Georg Wilhelm Friedrich Hegel uses geography to justify slavery and colonization of the African people. Hegel is important to us in understanding the issue of reparation. From his thoughts, we can see that European and Western concepts of Africa are highly subjective. Many of these old-time Western thinkers (to use a charitable word for them) used missionary stories of Africa to propound theories, even when they had never lived or visited Africa. For centuries, Western scholars continued to duplicate the distortions laid down by their predecessors to evaluate the African continent, according to the Kenyan-born historian Ali Mazrui.

According to Hegel, the world is divided into three regions, Artic, Tropical and Temperate. Hegel argues that Africans are still in the stage of humanity's childhood, so the people of Africa lack reason, wisdom, and the ability to fend for themselves. Hegel's reasoning says Africans live in the tropical region, which is very hot, making their human brains disinclined to create anything. To Hegel, the people of the temperate region are in search of objective knowledge that entails reflective and mature thinking. As a result, colonialism and slavery are, theoretically, morally and intellectually justified, since the black race is the burden of the white race. The idea of the three stages of human progress provides justification for the near-total extermination of the Native Americans, for slavery, and for colonialism. In summary, the three stages of Hegelian human development are childhood, ego, and reason.

So far, we have seen how Hegel generalizes about Africa based on false missionary information. Since Africa and the Developing Nations are left behind in the first stage of human development known as the childhood of humanity, Hegel argues that European nations can colonize and enslave Africa since God has given them the ego, reason, and wisdom to conquer and rule. Hegel further argues that the black people of the world were the burden of the white race. Hegel therefore confirms that European colonizers and slave traders stole Africa's civilization, religion, culture, arts and education.

Significance of Hegel's Philosophy of History

Hegel is very important in helping us to understand when the rain began to beat us, as we say in Africa – or, simply put, when the African problem began. First, his thesis provides theoretical, moral, and intellectual justification for destroying, dominating and/or repressing African people, and Native Americans as well. Native Americans had become redundant and could not effectively do plantation work: hence the need for African slaves. Surprisingly, Africans thrived and survived in the American plantations. Hegel did not know how to deal with this African strength and success where the Native Americans had failed. However, Hegel insisted that the liberal axiom, or democracy, had no place in Africa, since Africans were not capable of developing on their own.

It is now common knowledge that Hegel's philosophy rejects certain basic tenets of liberalism: for example, that all human beings are born with the capacity to reason. "We are rational beings only so far as we are partakers in ethical and social life," he argues.

Freedom is the ability to subordinate our passions to our thinking self. Hegel rejects the liberal conception of natural rights and social contract theory. Therefore, we have rights only if such rights are given by the State or those dictated by the rational will of States. Hegel believes that war is progressive and necessary. All colonial wars were a necessary development.

Horowitz: This is your idea? What about refugees and stateless people – do they have no rights? I don't understand why you're saying this.

Ewa: This is Hegel's idea, not mine.

Hegel Today

Hegel influences our society today in many ways, especially in the gap between rich American nation-state and poor African nation-states.

African political theories and thinkers dismiss and reject Hegel's theory and of Professor Hugh Trevor-Roper's own theoretical frameworks which are based on speculation and hearsay.

Is Professor Trevor-Roper Right or Wrong About Africa?

People are again talking about slavery and reparation. But it is a complex and difficult issue. How should America, Europe, and the traumatized societies deal with the unhealed past, especially when the perpetrators still imagine the post-slavery people as non-persons? According to Trevor-Roper, Africa has no history. It is a dark continent. And you cannot write a history of darkness.

Imagine Professor Trevor-Roper's claim that Africa has no history. Africa is "no historical part of the world; it has no movement or development to exhibit," Trevor-Roper writes. "There is only the history of Europeans in Africa. The rest is darkness ... the unedifying gyrations of barbarous tribes in picturesque but irrelevant corners of the globe."

However, another European, Theodore Canot, who worked as a slaver and slave ship captain for twenty years, contradicts Roper and Hegel.[31]

---

31   "Hugh Trevor-Roper." *Wikipedia*, en.wikipedia.org/wiki/Hugh_Trevor-Roper. Accessed

"I have no hesitation in saying that three-fourths of the slaves sent abroad from Africa are the fruit of wars fomented by the avarice of our own [white] race. We stimulate the Negro's passion by the introduction of wants and fancies never dreamed of by the simple native, while slavery in Africa was an institution of domestic need and custom alone. But what was once a luxury has now ripened into an absolute necessity; so that Man, in truth, has become the coin of Africa."

14 Nov. 2019.

25

SEEKING JUSTICE

Ifeanyi Chukwu – There is no power greater than God's power.
Africa before trans-Atlantic slavery

Many Europeans thought that Africa's history was not important. They argued that Africans were inferior to Europeans and they used this to help justify slavery. However, the reality is very different. A study of African history shows that Africa was by no means inferior to Europe. As you can see above, the people who suffered the most from the trans-Atlantic slave trade were civilized, organized, and technologically advanced people, long before the arrival of European slavers, trying to suggest they were backward people.

- Egypt was the first of many great African civilizations. It lasted thousands of years and achieved many magnificent and incredible things in the fields of science, mathematics, medicine, technology, and the arts. Egyptian civilization was already over 2000 years old by the time the city of Rome was built.
- In the west of Africa, the kingdom of Ghana was a vast empire that spread across an area the size of Western Europe. Between the ninth and thirteenth centuries, it traded in gold, salt and copper. It was like a medieval European empire, with a collection of powerful local rulers controlled by one king or emperor. Ghana was highly advanced and prosperous. It is said that the Ghanaian ruler had an army of 200,000 men.
- The kingdoms of Benin and Ife were led by the Yoruba people and sprang up between the 11th and 12th centuries. The Ife civilization goes back as far as 500BC and its people made objects from bronze, brass, copper, wood and ivory. Studies of the Benin show that they were highly skilled in ivory carving, pottery, and rope and gum production.
- From the thirteenth to the fifteenth century, the kingdom of Mali spread across much of West and North-East Africa. At its largest, the kingdom was 2000 kilometers wide and there was

an organized trading system, with gold dust and agricultural produce being exported north. Mali reached its height in the 14th century. Cowrie shells were used as a form of currency and gold, salt and copper were traded.

- Between 1450-1550, the Songhay kingdom grew very powerful and prosperous. It had a well-organized system of government and a currency, and it imported fabrics from Europe.
- Timbuktu became one of the most important places in the world. Libraries and universities were built, and it became a meeting place for poets, scholars and artists from other parts of Africa and the Middle East.

Forms of slavery existed in Africa before Europeans arrived. Some countries in the African continent had their own systems of slavery. People were enslaved as punishment for a crime or as payment for a debt, or because they were taken prisoner during wars. However, African slavery was different from what was to come later. In some kingdoms, temporary slavery could be imposed to punish criminals. In some cases, enslaved people could work to buy their freedom. Children of enslaved people did not automatically become slaves.

Students Seek Justice

On April 11, 2019 Georgetown students voted to pay a fee benefiting the descendants of enslaved people who were sold to pay off the school's debts. The referendum proposes a $27.20 fee added to the cost of attendance every semester at Georgetown University. "It's designated by five students and five descendants, who would be democratically elected. And they would utilize the funds to work on projects or initiatives meant to empower and support descendant communities.

In 1838, Georgetown University sold 272 enslaved people to pay off a debt. Over the last several years, there has been a reckoning on campus as the school wrestles with its ties to slavery. It renamed several buildings that had honored people involved in the slave trade. Some descendants of that original group of enslaved people are now enrolled at the university.

Controversies Today

To pay or not to pay. Should current government and society be held responsible for crimes committed 250 years ago? Is there any need to give more attention to slavery, which occurred centuries ago? Can reparations right the wrongs of today? What about Africa's complicity in the slave trade? Some people argue that we cannot repair the injustice of slavery while white supremacy grows on checked.

Sampled High School Students

Are we morally responsible to right the wrongs of our parents' generation?

"A lot of times we don't have a choice but to right those wrongs since they affect us today." –Tovar

"Yes, for certain things need to be changed if it is negatively impacting people." – Alicia

"No, but we are told we should." – Ethan

"In a way yes seeing as those well done, but you can't undo a wrong that is written into history, it stays there despite attempting to do good we are morally responsible to correct the wrong. Islas

That was their time. Now it is our time. They had their time; they chose to commit all those wrongs. We shouldn't be held responsible for their actions." – Vanessa

"No, because what happened in past generations is not our fault. We had nothing to do with their actions; we could not stop them or change them. There is and was nothing we could do." – Packer

"No, I believe we are not morally responsible to right the wrongs of our parents because I feel like if we did then, we wouldn't be able to experience our own right and wrong choices. I believe it is all about choices "because we don't have to be the same or similar to them." – Daniel

"Yes, we are responsible to correct the mistakes of our parents; for example, my dad is a little homophobic and it is my job to correct that behavior." – Nathan

"I don't believe we are responsible, but we can have a better outcome that we fix it. It is not fair for us to take responsibilities of our parents' wrong doings but being negative and not wanting to fix it won't make it better. It's easier to fix their wrongdoings to make life easier and less complex." – Karely

"No, we are not morally responsible to right our parents' wrongs because the mistakes they did in the past is their responsibility and they have to deal with the consequences because it is not my responsibility to fix it." – Suad

"I don't think we are morally responsible to right the wrongs of our parent generation because we are also still learning to understand what is right in some situations." – Jackeline

"No, but if we want a better future, we must do so to give future generations better than what we had." – Contreras

"We are responsible to right the wrongs of our last generations because we are living off the wrongs. It is our job to better our following generations over time." – Jimenez

"No, because we are different people with different beliefs, so what is wrong to me might not be wrong to them." – Giselle

"We are not, but we live in that world, so we have to help people feel comfortable instead of shaming like how our parents did. Example, being homosexual." – Adrian

"Yes, we are, because of them our generation is so messed up." – Cyana

Voices for Reparation

"The making of amends for a wrong one has to be done, by paying money to or otherwise help those who have been wronged." – Goodloe

"It should be paid to African Americans because we have been doing wrong for so long. We are still being treated differently till this day." – Anderson

"I feel like reparation should be paid to the African Americans because of the wrongs they did to us throughout the years. So

I do feel like making amends for a wrong which has been done by paying money." – Jamond

"Yes, African Americans should be paid reparation. I say yes because slavery is something that a human should never go through. If slavery would have never happened, most African Americans would be in Africa, our ancestors were robbed of their history." – Ahshantie

"Reparation should be paid. Slaves worked for free for hundreds of years without pay or recognition. The country was built on the backs of slaves and African Americans should get something for it instead of being cast aside." – Michael

"Yes, because Americans don't deserve credit for ending slavery on a paper. African Americans suffered and worked hard enough." – Blessing

"I believe that reparation should be paid to African Americans because they deserve that justice. Even if it wasn't them personally that suffer from slavery, their ancestors were put through all those sufferings and discriminations by white people. And that fact is not right because no men or women should ever be treated like the way they were for their differences." – Their

"I think that they should get reparation because everything that they have suffered and plus they will get an education they deserve. Reparation should have happened when slavery stopped." – Isadora

"I feel that when they are wronged then yes. Like when the police are being racist and is unfair, then yes. But with the slaves that should have been done a long time ago. No one today experienced what the slaves went through. If the slaves were still alive then yes, they deserve the money. But that time has passed, the slaves are all gone and so are the people responsible." – Trinity

"I am for reparation because even though, the people pass away, they should be given to their generations at least to be fair of what they had done to them." – Mary Tha

"Yes, because they deserve it after the years of being in pain and enslaved. I believe that anyone who has been treated like that should receive reparation. I think reparation for the African Americans should have been done a long time ago." – Sydney

"Yes, because they have earned it through their years of toil and involvement, how much they have contributed and given to the world." – Martin

"Of course, reparation should be paid to African-Americans. The hardship they went through is well deserved to be paid for like the adults always tells us, apologize to those you have done wrong. And so, we should follow that concept and apologize by paying them." – Phun[32]

---

32   Hegel and Trevor-Roper.

26

LONG-MUTED VOICES

Ilo Abu Chi – The person who hates me is not my God.

In 2020, compensating the descendants of American slaves suddenly resurfaced as a hot topic on the campaign trail, with the US presidential candidates voicing support for reparation. New proposals also seek financial redress for decades of legalized segregation and discrimination against African Americans in employment, housing, health and education.

But why now? And just how would reparations, focused specifically on slavery, work?

Here's what you need to know about this most controversial of subjects.

How do you put a cash value on hundreds of years of forced death and servitude?

This may be the most contested part. Academics, lawyers, and activists have given it a shot, though, and their results vary.

Most formulations have produced numbers from as low as $17 billion to as high as almost $5 trillion.

The most often-quoted figure, though, is truly staggering, as anthropologist and author Jason Hickel notes in his 2018 book, "The Divide: Global Inequality from Conquest to Free Markets:"[33]

"It is estimated that the United States alone benefited from a total of 222,505,049 hours of forced labor between 1619 and the abolition of slavery in 1865. Valued at the US minimum wage, with a modest rate of interest, that is worth $97 trillion today."

Keep in mind, the *total* US federal budget for fiscal year 2018 was $4.1 trillion.

Other formulations are more modest, like a 2015 report by University of Connecticut assistant professor Thomas Craemer. He estimated that the labor of slaves was worth at least $5.9 trillion and perhaps as much as $14.2 trillion (in 2009 dollars). Craemer came up with that figure by estimating the monetary value of slaves over time, the total number of hours they worked and the wages at which that work should have been compensated.

Craemer's number is also lower because he only deals with the slavery that happened from the time of the country's founding

---

33   Jason Hickel, 2018, "The Divide: Global Inequality from Conquest to Free Markets".

until the end of the Civil War, so it ignores slavery during the colonial period and the discrimination that blacks endured during the Jim Crow era.

Where would the money come from?

Generally, advocates for reparations say that three different groups should pay for them: governments, private companies and rich families that owe a good portion of their wealth to slavery.

It makes sense that **federal and state governments** (which enshrined, supported and protected the institution of slavery) and **private businesses** (which financially benefited from it), would be tempting targets from which reparations could be extracted. But **wealthy families?**

"There are huge, wealthy families in the South today that once owned a lot of slaves. You can trace all their wealth to the free labor of black folks. So, when you identify the defendants, there are a vast number of individuals," attorney Willie E. Gary told Harper's magazine in November 2000, during the height of the last, big time of reparations talk. Gray was talking about how these families could be sued for reparations since they benefited directly from slavery.

As you might imagine, suing large groups of people to pay for reparations wouldn't go over well. Others have suggested lawmakers could pass legislation to force families to pay up. But that might not be constitutionally sound.

"I don't think you can legislate and have those families pay," Malik Edwards, a law professor at North Carolina Central University, told CNN. "If you're going to go after individuals, you'd have to come up with a theory to do it through litigation. At least on the federal level Congress doesn't have the power to go after these folks. It just doesn't fall within its Commerce Clause powers."

The Commerce Clause refers to the section of the US Constitution which gives Congress the power to regulate commerce among the states.

But reparation means more than a cash payout

It could come in the form of special social programs. It could mean giving away land.

That's why people need to check the fine print on the support all of those Democratic presidential candidates have given to reparations. None of them has articulated a concrete proposal that would specifically give a cash benefit to black Americans.

They've talked about developing tax credits that would go to all low-income people, not just blacks, and creating so-called "baby bonds" that would help all of America's children pay for college, not just African American children.

None of the major Democratic candidates so far has proposed making direct cash payments to African Americans as a way for the country to atone for its "original sin," except for Marianne Williamson, who announced her candidacy in January.

Williamson, a best-selling author and spiritual counselor to Oprah Winfrey, has advocated for reparations for years and proposes giving $100 billion in reparations for slavery, with $10 billion a year to be distributed over 10 years.

Others have suggested a mix of cash and programs targeted to help African Americans.

"Direct benefits could include cash payments and subsidized home mortgages similar to those that built substantial white middle-class wealth after World War II but targeted to those excluded or preyed upon by predatory lending," Chuck Collins, an author and a program director at the Institute for Policy Studies, told CNN. "It could include free tuition and financial support at universities and colleges for first generation college students." Reparation funds could also be used to provide one-time endowments to start museums and historical exhibits on slavery, Collins said.

What are the arguments against reparations?

There are many. Opponents of reparations argue that all the slaves are dead, no white person living today owned slaves or that all the immigrants that have come to America since the Civil War don't have anything to do with slavery. Also, not all black people living in America today are descendants of slaves (like former President Barack Obama).

Others point out that slavery makes it almost impossible for most African Americans to trace their lineage earlier than the Civil War, so how could they prove they descended from enslaved people?

Writer David Frum noted those and other potential obstacles in a 2014 piece for *The Atlantic* entitled "The Impossibility of Reparations," which was a counterpoint to Coates' essay. Frum warned that any reparations program would eventually be expanded to other groups, like Native Americans, and he feared that reparations could create their own brand of inequality.

"Within the target population, will all receive the same? Same per person, or same per family? Or will there be adjustment for need? How will need be measured?" asks Frum, a former speechwriter for President George W. Bush. "And if reparations were somehow delivered communally and collectively, disparities of wealth and power and political influence within black America will become even more urgent. Simply put, when government spends money on complex programs, the people who provide the service usually end up with much more sway over the spending than the spending's intended beneficiaries."

In a recent column for The Hill, conservative activist Bob Woodson decried the idea of reparations as "yet another insult to black America that is clothed in the trappings of social justice." He also told CNN he feels America made up for slavery long ago, so reparations aren't needed.

"I wish they could understand the futility of wasting time engaging in such a discussion when there are larger, more important challenges facing many in the black community," Woodson, the founder and president of the Woodson Center, told CNN. "America atoned for the sin of slavery when they engaged in a civil war that claimed hundreds of thousands of lives. Let's for the sake of argument say every black person received $20,000. What would that accomplish?"

This isn't the first-time reparations have come up

After decades of languishing as something of a fringe idea, the call for reparations really caught steam in the late 1980s through the '90s.

Former Democratic Rep. John Conyers first introduced a bill in 1989 to create a commission to study reparations. Known as HR 40, Conyers repeatedly re-introduced the bill, which has never been passed, until he left office in 2017. Texas Democratic Rep. Sheila Jackson Lee has taken up the baton, sponsoring HR 40 in this year's Congress.

Activist groups, like the National Coalition of Blacks for Reparations in America and the Restitution Study Group, sprang up during this period. Books, like Randall Robinson's "The Debt: What America Owes to Blacks," gained huge buzz.

Then came the lawsuit. In 2002, Deadria Farmer-Paellmann became the lead plaintiff in a federal class-action suit against a number of companies – including banks, insurance company Aetna and railroad firm CSX – seeking billions for reparations after Farmer-Paellmann linked the businesses to the slave trade.

She got the idea for the lawsuit as she examined old Aetna insurance policies and documented the insurer's role in the 19th century in insuring slaves. The suit sought financial payments for the value of "stolen" labor and unjust enrichment and called for the companies to give up "illicit profits."

"These are corporations that benefited from stealing people, from stealing labor, from forced breeding, from torture, from committing numerous horrendous acts, and there's no reason why they should be able to hold onto assets they acquired through such horrendous acts," Farmer-Paellmann said at the time.

The case was tossed out by a federal judge in 2005 because it was deemed that Farmer-Paellmann and the other plaintiffs didn't have legal standing in the case, meaning they couldn't prove a sufficient link to the corporations or prove how they were harmed. The judge also said the statute of limitations had long since passed.

Appeals to the US 7th Circuit Court of Appeals and the US Supreme Court proved unsuccessful, and the push for reparations kind of petered out.

But Coates' 2014 article in *The Atlantic* reignited interest in the issue. New reparations advocacy groups, like the United States Citizens Recovery Initiative Alliance Inc., took up the fight. Black Lives Matter includes slavery reparations in its list of proposals to improve the economic lives of black Americans. Even a UN panel said the US should pay reparations.

And now major candidates for president are endorsing the idea.

So, what are the prospects of reparations moving forward?

Despite the words of support from these Democratic presidential candidates, slavery reparations still face an uphill battle.

The idea isn't popular with the American public. A 2016 Marist poll found that 68% of Americans don't think the US should pay reparations to the descendants of slaves. Unsurprisingly there's a racial divide to this. Some 81% of white Americans are against reparations, while 58% of African Americans support them. What is surprising is the generational divide the poll revealed. Millennials surveyed were much more likely than Baby Boomers or Gen-Xers to support reparations. Even still, a total of 49% of millennials opposed them.

Those numbers make it difficult for any candidate to try to sell a skeptical American public on the idea and to get lawmakers to pass legislation. And after the failure in the courts of Farmer-Paellmann's lawsuit more than a decade ago, taking legal action to secure reparations doesn't seem like the most promising route either.

Whatever happens, almost everyone agrees that something needs to be done to cut down the huge wealth gap between white and blacks that slavery helped to create. Collins, the author and scholar, said his own research showed that the median wealth of a white household is $147,000, which is about 41 times greater than the median wealth of a black family, which is $3,600.

"This can only be explained through an understanding of the multigenerational legacy of white supremacy in asset building," he told CNN.

"People say, 'slavery was so long ago' or 'my family didn't own slaves.' But the key thing to understand is that the unpaid labor of millions -- and the legacy of slavery, Jim Crow laws, discrimination in mortgage lending and a race-based system of mass incarceration -- created uncompensated wealth for individuals and white society as a whole. Immigrants with European heritage directly and indirectly benefited from this system of white supremacy. The past is very much in the present."[34]

---

34 Collins "The past is very much in the present."

27

PRESIDENTIAL CANDIDATES SPEAK

Ochi Ora – The King who rules or governs the people.

From right to left: Kamala Harris, Bernie Sanders, Julian Castro, Corey Booker, Elizabeth Warren and Olauda Equiano the emancipated African slave.

2019. It is election time in the United States and politicians are talking again about slavery, human rights and reparation. To the African American community, reparation for the trans-Atlantic slavery might be acceptable. However, reparation to Africa's most degraded daughters and sons, the Igbos, is a more complicated and thorny issue. While Eurocentric human rights, though well-meaning in intent, wrongly presents reparative justice as a universal prescription for post conflict healing and reconciliation, the Igbo-centric model seeks, first, spiritual atonement and freedom, not financial compensation. Igbos, also known as Biafran people, believe in *ifesinachi* - the concept that we live in a world of dualism, and as such, all good and bad karma come from God. Therefore, the trans-Atlantic slave trade is attributed to Igbo people's collective karma which needs to be dissolved.

In order to secure support from the African American community, the Democratic presidential candidates had been openly declaring their positions on the issue of reparative justice. While some candidates support the case for compensation to the descendants of the slaves, some candidates do not embrace the idea. While Senator Cory Booker, like Sheila Jackson Lee, introduces a senate companion version of the House bill in support of reparation payments, Senator Kamala Harris argues that reparation means "different things to different people," according to Khorri Atkinson.

Senator Bernie Sanders thinks the issue is quite "divisive." Mayor Julian Castro would create a committee to "study reparations," while Senator Amy Klobuchar believes "we have to invest in those communities that have been so hurt by racism...it doesn't have to be a direct pay for each person, but what we can do is to invest in those communities."

Senator Elizabeth Warren tweets in support of Jackson Lee's bill, arguing that, "slavery is a stain on America, and we need to address it."

While Senator Kirsten Gillibrand supports the study of reparation, she asserts, "This is a conversation that is long overdue."

Beto O'Rourke, like Bernie Sanders, is not quite interested in the issue of reparation. The most enthusiastic candidate so far is Marianne Williamson, who proposes $100 billion "a year to be distributed over 10 years for economic and educational projects."

In hindsight, neither Barack Obama nor Hillary Clinton supported the reparation question.[35]

35

28

DURBAN CONFERENCE

Igwe bu Ike – Unity is power.

In the last ten years, a worldwide movement has emerged for reparations to various previously subordinated groups for past wrongs. The first paper at the conference discusses the movement for reparations to the continent of Africa. It begins with a discussion of the United Nations-sponsored World Conference against Racism, Racial Discrimination, Xenophobia and Related Intolerance held in Durban, South Africa, in September 2001. It then traces the discussion of reparations to Africa back to the Group of Eminent Persons (GEP) established in the early 1990s by the Organization of African Unity to pursue reparations for slavery and (perhaps) other wrongs perpetrated on Africa.

At the Durban Conference against Racism, it was suggested that the Western world owed reparations to Africa. These reparations would be for the slave trade and colonialism, and even for the post-colonial era.

The Declaration issued as the Final Document of the Conference stated: "We acknowledge that slavery and the slave trade… are a crime against humanity, and should always have been so, especially the trans-Atlantic slave trade, and are among the major sources and manifestations of racism, racial discrimination, xenophobia and related intolerance… We recognize that colonialism has led to racism, racial discrimination, xenophobia and related intolerance." Moreover, the Declaration stated that victims of violations of their human rights as a result of racism and related wrongs should have "the right to seek just and adequate reparation or satisfaction."

Several African countries supported this claim. For example, Ali Mohamed Osman Yassin, Minister of Justice of Sudan, made a statement explicitly linking the slave trade to the current problems of Africa.

The Caribbean Reparation Commission

Discussions on the issue of Reparations for Native Genocide and Slavery were initiated at the Thirty-Fourth Regular Meeting of the Conference of Heads of Government of CARICOM in July 2013 in Trinidad and Tobago, following a proposal from the Prime Minister of St. Vincent and the Grenadines, Dr. the Hon. Ralph Gonsalves, to engage the United Kingdom and other former colonial European nations on the matter. The proposal of the Honorable Prime Minister was made against the backdrop of a book written by Professor Sir Hilary Beckles entitled "Britain's Black Debt: Reparations for Caribbean Slavery and Native Genocide".

At the inaugural discussions, Heads of Government expressed unanimous support for the initiative and defined a governance arrangement for its implementation. A Prime Ministerial

Sub-Committee (PMSC) on Reparations was established under the Chairmanship of the Prime Minister of Barbados and comprising the Chair of Conference and the Heads of Government of Guyana, Haiti, St. Vincent and the Grenadines and Suriname, to oversee the work of the Reparations Commission.

The Conference also agreed on the establishment of national reparations committees and a regional CARICOM Reparations Commission (CRC), constituted by chairpersons of the national committees. The Terms of Reference of the CRC specifies the main mandate of the Commission as to establish the moral, ethical and legal case for the payment of Reparations by the Governments of all the former colonial powers and the relevant institutions of those countries, to the nations and people of the Caribbean Community for the Crimes against Humanity of Native Genocide, the Trans-Atlantic Slave Trade and a racialized system of chattel Slavery.

The CRC, which is chaired by University of the West Indies Vice Chancellor Prof. Sir Hilary Beckles, first met in September 2013 in St. Vincent and the Grenadines. National Committees on Reparations have been established in 12 Member States to date. As at February 2016, National Reparations Committees have been established in the following Member States:

- Antigua and Barbuda
- The Bahamas
- Barbados
- Belize
- Dominica
- Guyana
- Jamaica
- St. Kitts and Nevis

- St. Lucia
- St. Vincent and Grenadines
- Suriname
- Trinidad and Tobago[36]

---

36   National Reparations Committees.

29

REPARATION PRECEDENTS

Mmefie Adiro Mgbaghalu ama di – If there is no injustice, there would be no forgiveness.

It seems American people and the global community are genuinely fine with reparative justice, just not for slavery. Such countries like Austria, France, South Africa, Canada and the United States of America have made efforts to deal with past wrongs in their country's history.

At the end of the Second World War, the USA assisted the Jewish victims of the Holocaust to demand reparative justice from Austria and Germany.

- Germany has paid billions of dollars in reparations for the unspeakable crimes committed in the name of the German people. In 2000, German President Johannes Rau apologized to Israel asking for forgiveness.
- In Japan, the government is more reluctant to

apologize for war crime atrocities. However, during the 1930s and the 1940s, many Asian and Korean women and girls were captured and forced into motels as sex slaves by Japanese soldiers. "Since the 1990s, Japan has faced growing international pressure for a formal apology and restitution to the so-called 'comfort women'." As recently as 2007, Japanese Prime Minister Shinzo Abe insisted that the Japanese military was not responsible for forcing the women into sexual slavery.

- According to Michael Sandel, other apology controversies involve historic injustices to indigenous peoples.
- In Australia, debate has raged in recent years over the government's obligation to the aboriginal people. From the 1910s to the early 1970s, aboriginal children were forcibly separated from their mothers and placed in white foster homes or settlement camps. The policy was to assimilate the children to white society and speed the disappearance of aboriginal culture. "DILEMMAS OF LOYALTY 209" [37]
- "As recently as 2016, the US Department of State helped Holocaust survivors access the payment owed to them by a French railways company that was an accomplice in deportations."

However, when it comes to reparation for the trans-Atlantic slavery, the politicians sweep the issue under the carpet and refuse to discuss it.

---

37 Annalisa Merelli, Has America paid reparations? - Quartz https://qz.com/1569005/has-america-paidreparations/.

Meanwhile, the debate seems to have been exhumed from the John Conyers' ashes of history. Reparations are surprisingly appearing in the platforms of the Democratic presidential candidates. "About 70% of Americans oppose them – white Americans are the least in favor of it. Reparation opponents point to practical concerns as a major impediment. Who would pay? Who has the right to be paid? Does everyone get the same amount?" (Merelli) p.3.[38]

These are easy questions to answer if there is a political will to take action on the reparation issue. "After all, reparations have been paid numerous times in the US at the federal, state and city levels- just not to descendants of slaves. Though slavery reparations would surpass those previously paid in amount and scope, their goal would be exactly the same."

The history of reparations payment reveals several instances in which the United States admitted acting wrongly and made atonement:

1. US to Japanese Americans
2. US to Aleuts of Alaska
3. North Carolina to eugenics victims
4. US to the victims of the Tuskegee experiment
5. Florida to the survivors of the Rosewood massacre
6. City of Chicago to victims of police torture

In the above cases, reparations were paid as financial compensations in recognition that an injustice had been done and that the debt had to be paid.

People who oppose reparations for slaves reject the idea that compensation should be paid to the descendants of the African

38

141

slaves who are still suffering from the horrors of slavery. If the politicians continue to talk about reparation, the doors to compensation might open up to African Americans though not to the Africans, even the Igbos, who suffered so much in the trans-Atlantic slave trade.[39]

39 Merelli, Annalisa. "Americans Are Totally Fine with Reparations, Just Not for Slavery." Quartz, 18 Mar. 2019, qz.com/1569005/has-america-paid-reparations/.

30

HISTORY OF REPARATION PAYMENTS

Echi dime – Tomorrow is pregnant. Nobody knows what tomorrow will deliver.

1990 U.S.A.	$ 1.2 Billion or $ 20,000 Each	JAPANESE AMERICANS
1990 AUSTRIA	$ 25 Million to Holocaust Survivors	JEWISH CLAIMS ON AUSTRIA
1988 CANADA	250,000 Sq. Miles of Land	INDIANS & ESKIMOS

1988 CANADA	$ 230 Million	JAPANESE CANADIANS
1986 U.S.A.	$ 32 Million 1836 Treaty	OTTAWAS OF MICHIGAN
1985 U.S.A.	$ 31 Million	CHIPPEWAS OF WISCONSIN

SOURCE[40]

40   Annalisa Merelli.

31

GLOBAL REPARATION MOVEMENTS

Ife diora nma – What maximizes the happiness of the society and minimizes society's pain.

E ver since slavery was abolished in the Caribbean in the 1830s and in the broader Americas in the 1860s and 1880s, the victims of slavery and their progeny have been struggling for justice to repair the damages wrought by this most horrific of crimes against humanity.

This struggle has ebbed and flowed over the decades of the 19th and 20th centuries but has always been consistent in the demands for restitution and recompense for the crimes of chattel slavery in the Western Hemisphere. Reparations have been part and parcel of other liberation movements over the years, i.e., the anti-colonial, anti-imperialist, Pan-Africanist, civil rights and human rights movements in North America,

Latin America and the Caribbean especially during the decades from the 1930s through the 1990s.

- The National Coalition of Blacks for Reparations in America (N'COBRA), a mass-based coalition organized for the sole purpose of obtaining reparations for African descendants in the United States, was launched in September 1987.
- N'COBRA defines reparations as a process of repairing, healing and restoring a people injured because of their group identity and in violation of their fundamental human rights by governments or corporations. Those groups that have been injured have the right to obtain from the government or corporation responsible for the injuries that which they need to repair and heal themselves. In addition to being a demand for justice, they argue that reparations is a principle of international human rights law.[41]

As we stated before, on January 1 2019, Congresswoman Sheila Jackson Lee reintroduced John Conyers' H.R. 40 Bill:

H.R.40 - Commission to Study and Develop Reparation Proposals for African-Americans Act 116th Congress (2019-2020)

Sponsor: Rep. Jackson Lee, Sheila [D-TX-18] (Introduced 01/03/2019)

Committees: House - Judiciary

---

41 http://www.ncobra.com/documents/history.html

Latest Action: House - 01/03/2019 Referred to the Subcommittee on the Constitution Civil Rights, and Civil Liberties.

Commission to Study and Develop Reparation Proposals for African-Americans Act

This bill establishes the Commission to Study and Develop Reparation Proposals for African-Americans. The commission shall examine slavery and discrimination in the colonies and the United States from 1619 to the present and recommend appropriate remedies. Among other requirements, the commission shall identify (1) the role of federal and state governments in supporting the institution of slavery, (2) forms of discrimination in the public and private sectors against freed slaves and their descendants, and (3) lingering negative effects of slavery on living African-Americans and society.

This landmark piece of legislation represented a crucial milestone in the long struggle for reparatory justice in America.

In 2001 at the UN's World Conference against Racism in Durban, South Africa, the demands for reparations featured prominently in the discussions and debates at this global forum.

Since the launch of the CARICOM Reparations Commission (CRC) in July, 2013, the global movement for reparatory justice has been re-energised and over the past three years the CRC has inspired the formation of the National African-American Reparations Commission, the European Reparations Commission and similar formations in Canada and Great Britain.

In April 2015, hundreds of reparations advocates from some 22 countries, including representatives from the CARICOM Reparations Commission, assembled in New York City for an International Reparations Conference organized by the US-based Institute of the Black World 21st Century.[42]

Since then, conversations and debates about reparations and reparatory justice have intensified across the world. Scholars and journalists in the USA, Europe and the Caribbean are now publishing more books and essays on these subjects than ever before.

Recent public opinion polls in the USA have indicated a substantial increase in the percentages of African-Americans and young white Americans who now support the call for reparations.

The State Legislature of Illinois passed a unanimous resolution calling on US President Barack Obama to use his executive authority to commission a study to detail the "economic impact" of enslavement and the failure of the nation to create a system that guaranteed equality to newly freed African descendants upon emancipation. In addition, the study would look at how others who received reparations in America have benefited from them and offer reparation proposals that address the legacy of enslavement among current African descendants in the areas of "education, employment, housing, health care and justice."

And, in the wake of the national conventions of both the Republican and Democratic Parties in the USA, a broad coalition associated with the Black Lives Matter movement released a platform of its own, demanding reparations and an

42   http://caricomreparations.org/the-global-reparationsmovement/.

"end to the wars against Black people." The list of demands from the Movement for Black Lives platform also includes the abolition of the death penalty, legislation to recognize the impacts of slavery, as well as investments in education initiatives, mental health services and employment programs.

The Reparations idea is resonating beyond the boundaries of the Caribbean and the United States. In early 2016, the prime minister of India said his country needs to examine seriously a claim for reparations for the suffering inflicted on the people of India from decades of British colonial rule prior to independence. The indigenous peoples of Australia and New Zealand are also voicing reparations demands, as are the large communities of African descent in Brazil and Colombia in Latin America.

By all objective indications, the global movement for reparations has turned a corner and will continue to strengthen and expand in the years ahead. In addition, the Chairman of the CARICOM Reparations Commission, Prof. Sir Hilary Beckles, has predicted that the movement for reparatory justice will become the greatest political and historical justice movement of the 21st Century.

Time has not healed the wounds of the trans-Atlantic slave trade. Although many societies worldwide have practiced one form of slavery or the other, the African version witnessed the global commodification of African men and women. Africa's most aggressive, intelligent, resilient and ultra-democratic ethnic Igbo nation is also the most brutalized, enslaved, and allegedly the most fraudulent. If Igbo people are considered fraudulent, can their criminal behavior be attributable to their traumatized past and long political exclusion? Experience shows that when a society is marginalized or excluded, such society will likely become poor and a breeding ground for crime and violence according to Rama Mani.

32

THE AROS, AMERICA, THE POPE, PORTUGAL, EUROPEAN CHURCHES, AND NATION STATES

Kaosiso Chukwu – As it pleases God.

Between the 1450s, when Pope Nicholas V approved the Portuguese practice of enslaving African "pagans and unbelievers," and the 1750s, when Aro traders kidnapped Ikwueno, the African slave trade became one of the largest economic enterprises in the world's history. It enriched the European nations whose merchants owned the ships, while it allowed some African people to grow powerful and to prey on others, and it brought labor to develop the Americas.

In 1750, few Europeans questioned either their right to enslave Africans or the economic benefits of doing so. By the 1780s, the high point of the African slave trade, when more than eighty-eight thousand Africans would be brought to the New World every year, the Atlantic slave trade was a well-established mercantile system connecting Africa, Europe, and the Americas in a web of commerce. *The Interesting Narrative*, p.8[43]

The undisputable truth, therefore, is that slave trade, which diminished the dignity of the enslaved Africans, was approved by the European and American churches and nation-states. The question then becomes whether or not the slave victims so abused and dispossessed, and their descendants are entitled to reparation.

Quakers And the World of Antislavery

In 1727, the Quakers boldly called the slave trade and slavery contrary to Christian ethics, even when some of them still owned and traded slaves. "Philadelphia Quaker Robert King bought Ikwueno to work in his slave-trading business. Ikwueno himself continued to work as a slave trader after he became free and in 1776 helped Charles Irving buy slaves for a Central American plantation. Slavery was a dominant feature of the eighteenth century, and nearly impossible to escape, as Ikwueno, John Annis, and George Whitefield learned." ibid p.8

The difficulty of imagining slavery is vividly demonstrated by the fact that even Olauda himself was also involved in the slave trade after obtaining his freedom. The Quakers, despite their humanitarian gestures, were also culpable. Slavery was at the center of Europe's economy during the 17th century. "England, Holland and France had become the leading slave traders, and their trade in slaves and sugar helped them become the world's leading economic power." Only very few ethical men and the slaves themselves could challenge the right of one man to enslave another man. Nobody would have imagined in 1750

---

43   ibid p.8.

that slavery in the Americas was entering its final century. During the 1780s, a massive campaign challenged the concept of slavery, such that in the 1790s, the slaves of Haiti, France's richest sugar colony, would successfully revolt against slavery.

Campaign to End Slavery

There are three major causes that brought about the end of slavery.

1. Evangelical Christianity
2. Persistent Quaker agitation
3. The American Revolution (1776-1783)

According to Olauda's narrative, "The rhetoric of liberty, however hypocritical, made it possible for Americans to insist on their own freedom while denying freedom to others. In 1773 slaves in Massachusetts petitioned the colonial assembly, a center for resistance to British authority, for their own freedom." ibid p.9[44]

According to Olauda, in 1787 the American Congress put an end to slavery within the territory North of the Ohio River. The new American constitution also allowed congress to end the slave trade after 1807. The American antislavery movement was influenced by diverse people: the Quakers, Baptists, and Methodists, free blacks, especially in cities like Boston, New York, and Philadelphia, slaves who challenged white authority by violence, by running away, or by simply resisting, and some revolutionaries who saw the inconsistency in basing their own freedom on the slavery of others. ibid p.10[45]

---

44   ibid p.9.
45   ibid p.10.

The Zong Massacre

In 1783, there was a case of mass murder which further exposed the horrors of slavery to the public. Olauda helped break the story of the killing of slaves in the ship known as *Zong*. The ship had left São Tomé along the West African coast in September of 1781 with 440 African slaves. About 2 months later, when the *Zong* had reached the Caribbean, sixty African slaves and seven crewmembers were dead. "Disease had ravaged the human cargo, while many of the surviving slaves were dying. The captain, thinking of the Liverpool owners and the dwindling profits, knew he could not sell even the remaining healthy slaves." Ibid p.11[46]

According to Olauda's narratives, the captain made a business decision. Since insurance would not pay for sick slaves killed by illness, he ordered fifty African slaves chained together and thrown overboard. The next day he ordered forty-two more drowned, and thirty-six on the third day. The captain sailed to England. When he arrived at Liverpool, the owners of *Zong* filed insurance claims for 132 drowned slaves.

This insurance claim might have been overlooked quietly except that Ikwueno "learned the true story." Ibid. Perhaps, a crewmember told him, which shows that even men who worked on slave ships had some conscience. When Ikwueno heard the story, he quickly alerted Granville Sharp, the British abolitionist, who was horrified, even though he knew the limits of British justice. British courts could not protect the slaves from their ship captain who had murdered them. "As Ikwueno would write of earthly courts, he saw 'no help in them, nor by the law.' The *Zong* massacre was a horrifying example of what happens when men and women are treated as property, and the

---

46   ibid p.11

British court's failure to do justice showed Ikwueno that laws made by men could not prevent the evils done by men." Ibid. The case of the *Zong* demonstrates man's inability to imagine others who are different.

Olauda Ikwueno's Legacy

As a free man, Olauda Ikwueno would eventually marry Susan Cullen, an English woman from Cambridge, who would die just few months after their second daughter Joanna's birth. Their first daughter, Anna Maria, had earlier died in April 1797.

While these antislavery advocates *imagined* and campaigned to set the slaves free, the advocates of reparation have not been as successful. As Humphrey Amaechina suggests, "My view is that we Africans should first apologize to ourselves before asking the white man to pay us for that tragic experience. Do you understand the law of karma...?" *See Appendix 1 for Humphrey's full letter.*

33

REPARATION TO AFRICA

Chineke Gbaghara – God forgive us.

According to Olauda and other slave narratives, the Igbo ethnic nation alone had over 75% of the trans-Atlantic slave trade. Igbo slaves were sold in Liverpool, London, West Indies, Virginia, Philadelphia, North and South Carolina, Alabama, New Orleans, Maryland and Georgia.

It is important to note that in 1789, Olauda was the first to publish an excellent description of his country, Biafra, before slavery and colonial invasion of Africa occurred. During that time, the African continent was making progress and developing its own unique government, commerce, social and cultural aspects of life, when slavery and colonization disrupted its growth and development.

"Our land is uncommonly rich and fruitful and produces all kinds of vegetables in great abundance. We have plenty of Indian corn and vast quantities of cotton and tobacco ...

all our work is exerted to improve these blessings of nature. Agriculture is our chief employment: and everyone even the children and women are engaged in it. The benefits of such a way of living are obvious. Those benefits are felt by us in the general healthiness of the people and in their vigor and activity." Slavery halted and destroyed this great African democratic experience and journey.

Igbo peoples' transitions from ancient times to colonial and slavery periods have damaged Igbo dignity, Igbo freedom and Igbo security. It is important to reiterate that when a society suffers from political exclusion, such society becomes poor, and poverty leads to crime and violence. Furthermore, such a society becomes a vulnerable zone for the recruitment of terrorists and other criminal gangs.

Igbo people, also known as Biafrans, are strong and resilient. Despite the Muslim massacre of Igbos in 1966, starvation, life in captivity and exclusion in Nigeria, Biafrans remain Africa's most aggressive, intelligent, resourceful people who had been forced to fight for survival. The wounds of the past have not healed, especially those of the trans-Atlantic slavery and of Igbo captivity in Nigeria as a conquered people.

As the debate on slavery is exhumed by American presidential candidates, what is the future of African Americans with or without reparation? What is also the future of Africans, especially Ndigbo? Is the sovereign Republic of Biafra possible?

From Slavery to Freedom

It has been an emotional and difficult journey of the Igbo people from slavery to colonization and from a federated Nigeria to the declaration of the Biafran Independence. We have also seen how Nigeria conquered and reannexed Biafra 50 years ago. The *Republic of Biafra* was a recognized State that existed for nearly 3 years before Nigeria defeated and forced the new Republic to rejoin Nigeria. Below are the details of the defunct Republic of Biafra.

34

REPUBLIC OF BIAFRA THE COUNTRY THE WORLD HAS FORGOTTEN

Ochichi

Ochichi – Power.
Ochichi - You have a traumatic history with mankind.
Ochichi – You made Esau to impersonate Jacob.
Ochichi – You made Pilate surrender Jesus Christ to his enemies.
Ochichi – You made Herod cut off John's head.
Ochichi – You made Goliath's head to be abandoned in the battlefield.
Ochichi – You made Pharoah's soldiers perish in the sea when they were chasing the Children of Israel.

When we were fighting the Biafra-Nigeria war, we made several vows to God.
We promised to become the children of Chineke if we survived.
But Chineke delivered us, and we forgot our promises and the words of our mouths.
Ochichi – You kill people, you make father and son to wage war against one another.

You make communities to turn against each other and to become enemies.
Ochichi – You waste money.
You are responsible for most of the conflicts and wars throughout the world today.

You've made Africa to become a continent perpetually in search of true freedom.
Ochichi - You killed Adolf Hitler of Germany.
Ochichi - You killed John F. Kennedy of America.
Ochichi - You killed Abraham Lincoln of America.
Ochichi - You are the nemesis of Kwame Nkrumah of Ghana.
Ochichi – You are responsible for laying our people in their graves.
During the Biafra-Nigeria war, many of us had no clothes to put on and no food to eat.
We lived in forests.

Ochichi – You drove us into the bush and drove us out of the bush.
We promised that if we survived, we would serve Chineke.
Ochichi – Those you drove into their graves have not risen, those you left with one leg are now using sticks as their second legs.
Those you have caused bodily injury are still lying on the floor, those you have selected to lead us have become corrupt and restless.
Those you've driven into prison have now understood that you are both sweet and bitter.

Ochichi, you build society, you destroy society, you destroy countries, you give wealth, but you corrupt minds with wealth.
Ochichi – You cast fear in people's mind.
Chineke delivered us but we have forgotten our covenant with Chineke.

The above song by F.U. OKWEY reveals the covenant and trust which the Igbo people have in Chineke – their Creation God, especially during the Biafra-Nigeria war.

Biafra's global campaign for recognition as a sovereign nation state has reached a critical stage such that if it is not resolved through diplomacy, it could lead to an unprecedented bloodbath or WWIII.

According to the Indigenous People of Biafra (IPOB) led by Mazi Nnamdi Kanu, the only reparation acceptable to Igbo people is the recognition of Biafra as de-jure, sovereign nation-state by the United Nations and the international community.

History

The **Republic of Biafra** is a juridical country in West Africa seeking recognition as an empirical state from the United Nations member states after 50 years since Nigeria conquered and annexed a sovereign nation by force.

Republic of Biafr
1967–1970

Flag

Coat of arms

Motto: "Peace, Unity, and Freedom."

Anthem: "Land of the Rising Sun"

Red: Republic of Biafra

Republic of Biafra in May 1967

Status: Unrecognized state
Capital: Enugu

Largest city: Aba
Common languages: English and Igbo (predominant)
French · Efik · Ekoi · Ibibio · Ijaw
Government: Republic
Historical era: Cold War
Established: 30 May 1967
Rejoins Federal Nigeria: 15 January 1970
Area: 77,306 km2 (29,848 sq mi)
1967 Population: 13,500,000
Currency: Biafran Pound

Biafra's declaration of independence from Nigeria resulted in civil war between Biafra and Nigeria. Biafra was formally recognized by Gabon, Haiti, Ivory Coast, Tanzania and Zambia. Other nations, which recognized Biafra by providing support and assistance to Biafra, include; Israel, France, Spain, Portugal, Norway, Rhodesia, South Africa and Vatican City. Biafra also received aid from non-state actors, including Joint Church Aid, Holy Ghost Fathers of Ireland, and under their direction Caritas International, and U.S. Catholic Relief Services. Médecins Sans Frontières (Doctors Without Borders) also originated in response to the suffering.

Its inhabitants were mostly Igbo, who led the secession due to economic, ethnic, cultural and religious tensions among the various peoples of Nigeria. Other ethnic groups within the Biafran Republic were; the Efik, Ibibio, Annang, Ejagham, Eket, Ibeno and the Ijaw among others.

After two-and-a-half years of war, during which almost two million Biafran civilians died from starvation caused by the total blockade of the region by the Nigerian and British governments, Biafran forces under Nigeria's motto of "No-victor, No-vanquished" surrendered to the Nigerian Federal

Military Government (FMG). The surrender was facilitated by the Biafran Vice President and Chief of General Staff, Major General Philip Effiong who assumed leadership of the Republic of Biafra after Colonel Chukwuemeka Odumegwu Ojukwu fled to Ivory Coast.

After the forced surrender of Biafra, some Igbos who had fled the conflict returned to their properties but were unable to get them back from their new occupants. This became law in the Abandoned Properties Act (28 September 1979). It was purported that at the start of the civil war, Igbos withdrew their money from Nigerian banks and converted it to the Biafran currency. After the war, bank accounts owned by Biafrans were seized and a Nigerian panel resolved to give every Igbo person with an account only 20 pounds. Today, Federal projects in Biafra are also greatly reduced compared to other parts of Nigeria. In an Intersociety study it was found that Nigerian security forces also extorted approximately $100 million per year from illegal roadblocks and other methods from Igboland, a cultural sub-region of Biafra in what is now southern Nigeria.[47]

---

47 https://en.wikipedia.org/wiki/Biafra#:~:text=Biafra%2C%20officially%20the%20Republic%20of,the%20Eastern%20Region%20of%20Nigeria.

35

AFRICA TODAY

Akwa Akwuru – Resilient Africa – Africa Awakening.

While an empirical state is capable of carrying out the minimal duties of maintaining law and order, providing general welfare to the people, a juridical state is recognized at the United Nations but has little or no capacity to enforce its domestic laws nor to provide the minimum needs of the people. The problem of Africa today is how to make the African juridical states into empirical states. However, Africa is not completely a piece of bad news. There is hope in the future of Africa. The continent has 54 nation-states, with a total population of over 600 million. As humanity's original home, Africa has the ancient roots of the three biggest monotheistic religions, Judaism, Christianity, and Islam. As a multi-religious continent, it has a high degree of heterogeneity and ethnicity. All the above attributes constitute the potential power of Africa. However, the great potential power of the continent, arising from its abundant human and natural resources, cannot guarantee peace and security, economic development, and happiness. As a continent that has experienced colonialism and the trans-Atlantic slave trade, Africa has not been able to transform itself from a mere juridical to an empirical continent. Until the future is founded on strategic memory and retroactive morality, Africa will likely remain in a perpetual state of flux – no stability and needs reconfiguration from virtual to real and viable nation-states.

Reflecting on the African condition, today, my assumption is that most of the 54 countries are mere flag democracies. Africa's nation states have not been capable to transform themselves from juridical to empirical states because of the continent's long history of collective and individual Kamenu or karma. Africa is not yet free to build an enduring and viable political, socio-economic state system and institutions.

In Africa's virtual democracy, the state looks real, but it is not. In the 54 countries, it appears they have real functional political institutions like the judiciary, legislature and the executive branches of government, but such institutions do not represent the real choices and interests of the African people. In these states, there is no accountability.

Africa, despite its potential power, is dealing with domestic and global conglomerate forces, especially the complex and thorny issue of slavery and reparation.

Reparative Justice: Compensation to the trans-Atlantic slave trade victims, although well-intended, is indeed misconceived and flawed. First, past and present debates focus on financial compensation and ignore the spiritual side of reparation. Second, Africa's exclusion from the reparative debate is an unfinished business. Third, so far, advocates have not been able to put a human face (like Olauda and his sister) on the reparation question. There is a general feeling that the past should be left alone while others feel that the past is a prelude to the future. Financial compensation alone cannot cleanse bloodguilt and Karma involved in these tragedies of slavery.

On September 30, 2005, I interviewed Ogugua Anonobi, an Igbo professor at Lincoln University, Missouri, on the evil of slavery and the complex issue of reparation.

"The world is imperfect by design. We live in a world of *osondi owendi* (happiness and misery) - a world of duality such as birth and death, crime and virtue, love and hate. The sun rises and sets, light and darkness, joy and sadness, success and failure. Reparation has three primary ramifications: economic, political and spiritual." Ogugua concluded, "There are things we can change and things we cannot change." To further put a face to the slavery reparative justice debate, let us listen to Olauda Ikwueno, the first African slave to write a book on the trans-Atlantic slave trade. Slave narratives are powerful indictments of the horrors of slavery and human rights abuses.

In **Life of Nobody**, my goal is to create a platform for the voices of freedom and reparation to restore the dignity of man and woman regardless of race or creed or gender. Abraham Lincoln's legacies are the Civil War and the Emancipation of enslaved Africans in the United States. Ralph Bunche will forever be remembered for the de-colonization of Africa with a stroke of his pen while my Igbo kinsman, Olauda Ikwueno's epic book and ideas helped to abolish slave trade in the UK by an Act of Parliament in 1807. Therefore, in re-imagining Olauda, we see an Igbo teenager who was forced into slavery but whose ideas played great roles in changing people's minds toward slave trading. Olauda's life is the Life of Somebody, Mkparawa - a gentle man, honest, hero.

Like Lincoln, Bunche and Olauda, there would be no greater legacy than for Joe Biden and Kamala Harris to be remembered for the Reparation Payment *proclamation.*

36

FUTURE

Nkiruka – The future is greater.

The past has refused to lie down quietly and heal. Olauda's epic book – *The Interesting Narrative of the Life of Olauda Equiano* is more than a slave's narrative. It is a story of one Igbo man's brutal encounter in this world, but who survives both physically and spiritually. Olauda's story is very important as the link between the past and the future. He has led us from the evil path of the *Aro underground railroad* to a new future of freedom that leads Africa from powerlessness to power. Transition to a more durable peace and security must be based on the rule of law and not on the rule of guns and hate.

Horowitz and I strongly suggest that the post-conflict society and government should establish *Truth and Reconciliation Commissions* in order to overcome the painful and violent past. Transitional justice experts work in partnership with societies, organizations and governments in post-conflict regions of the world. Victims of human rights abuses should speak out loud like Olauda to seek remedy. Such *Truth and Reconciliation Commissions* must include four important elements:

Truth: to establish the facts about violations of human rights that occurred in the past.

Justice: to investigate past violations and prosecute the suspected perpetrators.

Reparation: to provide relief to the victims and their families, including restitution, compensation, rehabilitation and guarantees of *odobeme*, non-repetition.

Inescapable law: Kamenu, an Ezza transitional justice mechanism is also known as the inescapable law of cause and effect. Unlike our constitutional laws, nobody can bypass or manipulate Kamenu. If any individual or society or government chooses to ignore Kamenu or karma, the forces of action and reaction will continue to control our lives, whether we believe it or not. We can see from Olauda's *Interesting Narrative*, that he was an Igbo prince, an abolitionist and mkparawa – a dignified and virtuous person. Most Africans at home and in diaspora are mkparawa.

Reparation to Africa vs The Law of Karma

Every society and every generation would have to reckon with the injustices of the past. Depending on each society's level of spiritual consciousness, leaders can utilize any transitional justice mechanism of their choice to heal the past and to reconcile society. Such mechanisms include Truth Commissions, International Criminal Courts, Gacaca, and Kamenu, depending on each society's own priorities such as – reconciliation, punishment, pardon or national recovery. The post-George Floyd and Breonna Taylor activists cannot rest until monetary reparation is paid especially in the USA.

On the contrary, the Ezza ethnic nation (Olauda and my homeland) would not likely seek financial reparation for the human rights abuses of our kinsmen and women during slavery. To us as Kamenuists, financial reparation is blood money entangled with blood guilt and Karma. Rather, Ezza people will first of all apologize to their African American relatives, fellow Africans and the entire African diaspora before seeking reparation for our kinsmen's unpaid labor during and after slavery.

The lives of Harriet Tubman, Ralph Bunche, Malcolm X, Martin Luther King, W.E.B DuBois, Barack Obama, Kamala Harris, Breonna Taylor and George Floyd are not the lives of nobody when we reimagine their contributions in building the foundation for a more prosperous and peaceful world. #iammkparawa.

WORKS CITED

1. Ndu Life Njoku, The Dual Image of the Aro – JORA 2015
2. p.88 The Interesting Narrative…edited by Robert. J. Allison 1995 Bedford Books, Boston.
3. Robert J. Allison, Igbo spiritual universe. p.5.
4. Olauda p.86.
5. Mark Tutton, CNN, 09/ 20, 2017.
6. Equiano ibid p. 5.
7. Ibid p.186.
8. *By Adaobi Tricia Nwaubani* Updated Sept. 20, 2019.
9. ibid p.190.
10. https://news.un.org/en/story/2018/12/1027271.
11. http://www.slaverysite.com/Body/facts%20 and%20figures.htm.
12. http://www.slaverysite.com/Body/facts%20 and%20figures.htm.
13. http://www.slaverysite.com/Body/facts%20 and%20figures.htm.
14. Source:https://en.wikipedia.org/wiki/Igbo_ people_in_the_Atlantic_slave_trade.
15. Ibid p.56.
16. According to Paul Thomas and Victor Ambrus, the authors of Olaudah Equiano from slavery to freedom p.34, 2007. Published by Collins, London.

17. 1865- Slavery is abolished in the United States at the end of the American Civil War.

18. https://commons.wikimedia.org/wiki/File:Slave_route.jpg.

19. https://commons.wikimedia.org/wiki/File:Slave_route.jpg.

20. https://caricomreparations.org/caricom/caricoms-10-point-reparation-plan.

22. https://www.stabroeknews.com/2019/10/22/news/regional/jamaica/former-jamaican-pm-pj-patterson-released-from-hospital-after-car-accident/.

23. https://www.stabroeknews.com/2019/10/22/news/regional/jamaica/former-jamaican-pm-pj-patterson-released-from-hospital-after-car-accident/ .

24. Nathaniel Horowitz.

25. Ahshantie.

26. Riley.

27. Humphrey Amaechina's last letter to Ewa Unoke.

28. Humphrey Amaechina's last letter to Ewa Unoke.

29. The life of Olaudah Equiano p.7.

30. The Life of Olaudah Equiano p.5.

31. https://thesource.com/2018/04/04/one-line-from-mlk-jr-s-letter-from-a-birmingham-jail-lives-through-blm/ .

32. Hegel and Trevor-Roper.

33. Voices for Reparations.

34. Jason Hickel, 2018, "The Divide: Global Inequality from Conquest to Free Markets".

35. Collins "The past is very much in the present."

36. Barack Obama nor Hillary Clinton supported the reparation question.

37. National Reparations Committees.

38. Annalisa Merelli, Has America paid reparations? - Quartz https://qz.com/1569005/has-america-paid-reparations/ .

39. Annalisa Merelli, p.3.

40. Annalisa Merelli.

41. http://www.ncobra.com/documents/history.html .

42.http://caricomreparations.org/the-global-reparations-movement/ .

43. Prof. Sir Hilary Beckles.

44. The Interesting Narrative.

45. ibid p.8.

46. ibid p.9.

47. ibid p.10.

48. ibid p.11.

49. https://en.wikipedia.org/wiki/Biafra#:~:text=Biafra%2C%20officially%20the%20Republic%20of,the%20Eastern%20Region%20of%20Nigeria.

50. The Interesting Narrative by Robert J. Allison p.11.

APPENDIX 1

Humphrey Amaechina's Last Letter

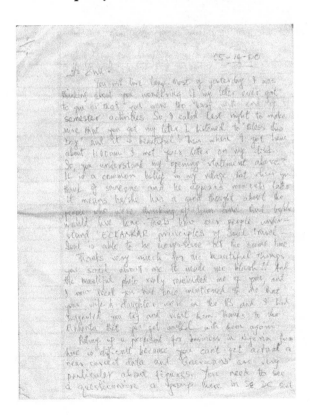

③

what I have in mind for your university is to
convince the Provost to allow us set up a
small business consulting unit, and a ceramic
making division in their fine arts dept. This
dept can make all the plates, cups etc used by
govt here hospitals & hotels in the state
and should be able to sell to the public. I
am thinking of writing a firms I saw in
the papers here for co-operation agreement,
there are so many things that we can do, but
we have to start gradually and build up into
a huge industrial group. Tried old contacts
all of food—what next while you are studying
what I am to now is to write a good
book ON REPARATION TO AFRICA. You may
remember that the late chief Abiola started talking
about it organising seminars both in Nigeria and
here to win peoples' support. But I was very
much against him— I tried to reach him on
the phone to discuss but failed. Then I
wrote him a long (2,5 pages) but-step letter
detailing my views. I never heard from
him, may be the letter didn't get to him.
briefly, my view was that we Africans should
first apologise to ourselves before asking
the whole world to pay us for the tragic
experience. You understand the laws of karma.
I gave him about three examples of black
angel against us (black Africans) here. that is so

APPENDIX 2

**Author's note: With Permission from *Project Gutenberg
Ebook*, We Reproduce Chapter 1 of Olauda's Book as
Evidence that Olauda is from Ezza.**

Olauda gives account of his Igbo "country" which existed
long before the US got independence in 1776 and the British
Amalgamation in 1914.

*On 30, May 1967, the ancient Igbo country was renamed **Biafra**.*

*Past narratives on Olaudah's alleged hometown in Igboland have
been dubious. Olauda, most logically is from Abakaliki, comprising
of Ezza, Izzi and Ikwo. More than any other Igbo community, the
trio are very famous for their agricultural skills, warrior culture,
superstition and the fear of poisoning. Olauda also describes Ezza
people's [Eke] market which was the center of the West African
slave trade. Olauda was born at Essaka (Ishieke) in Ezza–Izzi–
Ikwo. The name Ezaka is a popular name currently in Olauda's
homeland – my home too.*

*The civilized culture, vast agriculture and faith in One Creator are
all attributes of the Abakaliki and Ebonyi people in general.*

CHAPTER I.

EZZA A-Z

FROM OLAUDA'S OWN ACCOUNT

THE
INTERESTING NARRATIVE
OF
THE LIFE
OF
OLAUDAH EQUIANO,
OR
GUSTAVUS VASSA,
THE AFRICAN.

WRITTEN BY HIMSELF.

The author's [Olauda]account of his country, and their manners and customs—Administration of justice—Embrenche—Marriage ceremony, and public entertainments—Mode of living—Dress—Manufactures Buildings—Commerce—Agriculture—War and religion—Superstition of the natives—Funeral ceremonies of the priests or magicians—Curious mode of discovering poison—Some hints concerning the origin of the author's countrymen, with the opinions of different writers on that subject.

I believe it is difficult for those who publish their own memoirs to escape the imputation of vanity; nor is this the only disadvantage under which they labour: it is also their misfortune, that what is uncommon is rarely, if ever, believed, and what is obvious we are apt to turn from with disgust, and to charge the writer with impertinence. People generally think those memoirs only worthy to be read or remembered which abound in great or striking events, those, in short, which in a high degree excite either admiration or pity: all others they consign to contempt and oblivion. It is therefore, I confess, not a little hazardous in a private and obscure individual, and a stranger too, thus to solicit the indulgent attention of the public; especially when I own I offer here the history of neither a saint, a hero, nor a tyrant. I believe there are few events in my life, which have not happened to many: it is true the incidents of it are numerous; and, did I consider myself an European, I might say my sufferings were great: but when I compare my lot with that of most of my countrymen,

I regard myself as a *particular favourite of Heaven,* and acknowledge the mercies of Providence in every occurrence of my life. If then the following narrative does not appear sufficiently interesting to engage general attention, let my motive be some excuse for its publication. I am not so foolishly vain as to expect from it either immortality or literary reputation. If it affords any satisfaction to my numerous friends, at whose request it has been written, or in the smallest degree promotes the interests of humanity, the ends for which it was undertaken will be fully attained, and every wish of my heart gratified. Let it therefore be remembered, that, in wishing to avoid censure, I do not aspire to praise.

That part of Africa, known by the name of Guinea, to which the trade for slaves is carried on, extends along the coast above 3400 miles, from the Senegal to Angola, and includes a variety of kingdoms. Of these the most considerable is the kingdom of Benen, both as to extent and wealth, the richness and cultivation of the soil, the power of its king, and the number and warlike disposition of the inhabitants. It is situated nearly under the line, and extends along the coast about 170 miles, but runs back into the interior part of Africa to a distance hitherto I believe unexplored by any traveller; and seems only terminated at length by the empire of Abyssinia, near 1500 miles from its beginning. This kingdom is divided into many provinces or districts: in one of the most remote and fertile of which, called Eboe, I was born, in the year 1745, in a charming fruitful vale, named Essaka. The distance of this province from the capital of Benin and the sea coast must be very considerable; for I had never heard of white men or Europeans, nor of the sea: and our subjection to the king of Benin was little more than nominal; for every transaction of the government, as far as my slender observation extended, was conducted by the chiefs or elders of the place. The manners and government of a people who have little commerce with other countries are generally very simple; and the history of what passes in one family or village may serve as a specimen of a nation.

My father was one of those elders or chiefs I have spoken of, and was styled Embrenche; a term, as I remember, importing the highest distinction, and signifying in our language a *mark* of grandeur. This mark is conferred on the person entitled to it, by cutting the skin across at the top of the forehead, and drawing it down to the eye-brows; and while it is in this situation applying a warm hand, and rubbing it until it shrinks up into a thick *weal* across the lower part of the forehead. Most of the judges and senators were thus marked; my father had long born it: I had seen it conferred on one of my brothers, and I was also *destined* to receive it by my parents. Those Embrence, or chief men, decided disputes and punished crimes; for which purpose they always assembled together. The proceedings were generally short; and in most cases the law of retaliation prevailed. I remember a man was brought before my father, and the other judges, for kidnapping a boy; and, although he was the son of a chief or senator, he was condemned to make recompense by a man or woman slave.

Adultery, however, was sometimes punished with slavery or death; a punishment which I believe is inflicted on it throughout most of the nations of Africa[A]: so sacred among them is the honour of the marriage bed, and so jealous are they of the fidelity of their wives. Of this I recollect an instance:—a woman was convicted before the judges of adultery, and delivered over, as the custom was, to her husband to be punished. Accordingly he determined to put her to death: but it being found, just before her execution, that she had an infant at her breast; and no woman being prevailed on to perform the part of a nurse, she was spared on account of the child. The men, however, do not preserve the same constancy to their wives, which they expect from them; for they indulge in a plurality, though seldom in more than two. Their mode of marriage is thus:—both parties are usually betrothed when young by their parents, (though I have known the males to betroth themselves). On this occasion a feast is prepared, and the bride and bridegroom stand up in the midst of all their friends, who are assembled for the purpose, while he declares she is thenceforth to be looked upon as his wife, and that no other person is to pay any addresses to her.

This is also immediately proclaimed in the vicinity, on which the bride retires from the assembly. Some time after she is brought home to her husband, and then another feast is made, to which the relations of both parties are invited: her parents then deliver her to the bridegroom, accompanied with a number of blessings, and at the same time they tie round her waist a cotton string of the thickness of a goose-quill, which none but married women are permitted to wear: she is now considered as completely his wife; and at this time the dowry is given to the new married pair, which generally consists of portions of land, slaves, and cattle, household goods, and implements of husbandry. These are offered by the friends of both parties;

besides which the parents of the bridegroom present gifts to those of the bride, whose property she is looked upon before marriage; but after it she is esteemed the sole property of her husband. The ceremony being now ended the festival begins, which is celebrated with bonefires, and loud acclamations of joy, accompanied with music and dancing.

We are almost a nation of dancers, musicians, and poets. Thus every great event, such as a triumphant return from battle, or other cause of public rejoicing is celebrated in public dances, which are accompanied with songs and music suited to the occasion. The assembly is separated into four divisions, which dance either apart or in succession, and each with a character peculiar to itself. The first division contains the married men, who in their dances frequently exhibit feats of arms, and the representation of a battle. To these succeed the married women, who dance in the second division. The young men occupy the third; and the maidens the fourth. Each represents some interesting scene of real life, such as a great achievement, domestic employment, a pathetic story, or some rural sport; and as the subject is generally founded on some recent event, it is therefore ever new. This gives our dances a spirit and variety which I have scarcely seen elsewhere[B]. We have many musical instruments, particularly drums of different kinds, a piece of music which resembles a guitar, and another much like a stickado. These last are chiefly used by betrothed virgins, who play on them on all grand festivals.

As our manners are simple, our luxuries are few. The dress of both sexes is nearly the same. It generally consists of a long piece of callico, or muslin, wrapped loosely round the body, somewhat in the form of a highland plaid. This is usually dyed blue, which is our favourite colour. It is extracted from a berry, and is brighter and richer than any I have seen in Europe.

Besides this, our women of distinction wear golden ornaments; which they dispose with some profusion on their arms and legs. When our women are not employed with the men in tillage, their usual occupation is spinning and weaving cotton, which they afterwards dye, and make it into garments. They also manufacture earthen vessels, of which we have many kinds. Among the rest tobacco pipes, made after the same fashion, and used in the same manner, as those in Turkey[C].

Our manner of living is entirely plain; for as yet the natives are unacquainted with those refinements in cookery which debauch the taste: bullocks, goats, and poultry, supply the greatest part of their food. These constitute likewise the principal wealth of the country, and the chief articles of its commerce. The flesh is usually stewed in a pan; to make it savoury we sometimes use also pepper, and other spices, and we have salt made of wood ashes. Our vegetables are mostly plantains, eadas, yams, beans, and Indian corn. The head of the family usually eats alone; his wives and slaves have also their separate tables. Before we taste food we always wash our hands: indeed our cleanliness on all occasions is extreme; but on this it is an indispensable ceremony. After washing, libation is made, by pouring out a small portion of the food, in a certain place, for the spirits of departed relations, which the natives suppose to preside over their conduct, and guard them from evil.

They are totally unacquainted with strong or spirituous liquours; and their principal beverage is palm wine. This is gotten from a tree of that name by tapping it at the top, and fastening a large gourd to it; and sometimes one tree will yield three or four gallons in a night. When just drawn it is of a most delicious sweetness; but in a few days it acquires a tartish and more spirituous flavour: though I never saw any one intoxicated by it. The same tree also produces nuts and oil. Our principal luxury is in perfumes; one sort of these is an odoriferous wood of delicious fragrance: the other a kind of earth; a small portion of which thrown into the fire diffuses a most powerful odour[D]. We beat this wood into powder, and mix it with palm oil; with which both men and women perfume themselves.

In our buildings we study convenience rather than ornament. Each master of a family has a large square piece of ground, surrounded with a moat or fence, or enclosed with a wall made of red earth tempered; which, when dry, is as hard as brick. Within this are his houses to accommodate his family and slaves; which, if numerous, frequently present the appearance of a village. In the middle stands the principal building, appropriated to the sole use of the master, and consisting of two apartments; in one of which he sits in the day with his family, the other is left apart for the reception of his friends. He has besides these a distinct apartment in which he sleeps, together with his male children.

On each side are the apartments of his wives, who have also their separate day and night houses. The habitations of the slaves and their families are distributed throughout the rest of the enclosure. These houses never exceed one story in height: they are always built of wood, or stakes driven into the ground, crossed with wattles, and neatly plastered within, and without. The roof is thatched with reeds. Our day-houses are left open at the sides; but those in which we sleep are always covered, and plastered in the inside, with a composition mixed with cow-dung, to keep off the different insects, which annoy us during the night.

The walls and floors also of these are generally covered with mats. Our beds consist of a platform, raised three or four feet from the ground, on which are laid skins, and different parts of a spungy tree called plaintain. Our covering is calico or muslin, the same as our dress. The usual seats are a few logs of wood; but we have benches, which are generally perfumed, to accommodate strangers: these compose the greater part of our household furniture. Houses so constructed and furnished require but little skill to erect them. Every man is a sufficient architect for the purpose. The whole neighbourhood afford their unanimous assistance in building them and in return receive, and expect no other recompense than a feast.

As we live in a country where nature is prodigal of her favours, our wants are few and easily supplied; of course we have few manufactures. They consist for the most part of calicoes, earthern ware, ornaments, and instruments of war and husbandry. But these make no part of our commerce, the principal articles of which, as I have observed, are provisions. In such a state money is of little use; however we have some small pieces of coin, if I may call them such. They are made something like an anchor; but I do not remember either their value or denomination. We have also markets, at which I have been frequently with my mother.

These are sometimes visited by stout mahogany-coloured men from the south west of us: we call them Oye-Eboe, which term signifies red men living at a distance. They generally bring us fire-arms, gunpowder, hats, beads, and dried fish. The last we esteemed a great rarity, as our waters were only brooks and springs. These articles they barter with us for odoriferous woods and earth, and our salt of wood ashes. They always carry slaves through our land; but the strictest account is exacted of their manner of procuring them before they are suffered to pass. Sometimes indeed we sold slaves to them, but they were only prisoners of war, or such among us as had been convicted of kidnapping, or adultery, and some other crimes, which we esteemed heinous. This practice of kidnapping induces me to think, that, notwithstanding all our strictness, their principal business among us was to trepan our people. I remember too they carried great sacks along with them, which not long after I had an opportunity of fatally seeing applied to that infamous purpose.

Our land is uncommonly rich and fruitful, and produces all kinds of vegetables in great abundance. We have plenty of Indian corn, and vast quantities of cotton and tobacco. Our pine apples grow without culture; they are about the size of the largest sugar-loaf, and finely flavoured. We have also spices of different kinds, particularly pepper; and a variety of delicious fruits which I have never seen in Europe; together with gums of various kinds, and honey in abundance.

All our industry is exerted to improve those blessings of nature. Agriculture is our chief employment; and every one, even the children and women, are engaged in it. Thus we are all habituated to labour from our earliest years. Every one contributes something to the common stock; and as we are unacquainted with idleness, we have no beggars. The benefits of such a mode of living are obvious. The West India planters prefer the slaves of Benin or Eboe to those of any other part of Guinea, for their hardiness, intelligence, integrity, and zeal. Those benefits are felt by us in the general healthiness of the people, and in their vigour and activity; I might have added too in their comeliness.

Deformity is indeed unknown amongst us, I mean that of shape. Numbers of the natives of Eboe now in London might be brought in support of this assertion: for, in regard to complexion, ideas of beauty are wholly relative. I remember while in Africa to have seen three negro children, who were tawny, and another quite white, who were universally regarded by myself, and the natives in general, as far as related to their complexions, as deformed. Our women too were in my eyes at least uncommonly graceful, alert, and modest to a degree of bashfulness; nor do I remember to have ever heard of an instance of incontinence amongst them before marriage. They are also remarkably cheerful. Indeed cheerfulness and affability are two of the leading characteristics of our nation.

Our tillage is exercised in a large plain or common, some hours walk from our dwellings, and all the neighbours resort thither in a body. They use no beasts of husbandry; and their only instruments are hoes, axes, shovels, and beaks, or pointed iron to dig with. Sometimes we are visited by locusts, which come in large clouds, so as to darken the air, and destroy our harvest. This however happens rarely, but when it does, a famine is produced by it. I remember an instance or two wherein this happened. This common is often the theatre of war; and therefore when our people go out to till their land, they not only go in a body, but generally take their arms with them for fear of a surprise; and when they apprehend an invasion they guard the avenues to their dwellings, by driving sticks into the ground, which are so sharp at one end as to pierce the foot, and are generally dipt in poison.

From what I can recollect of these battles, they appear to have been irruptions of one little state or district on the other, to obtain prisoners or booty. Perhaps they were incited to this by those traders who brought the European goods I mentioned amongst us. Such a mode of obtaining slaves in Africa is common; and I believe more are procured this way, and by kidnapping, than any other[E]. When a trader wants slaves, he applies to a chief for them, and tempts him with his wares. It is not extraordinary, if on this occasion he yields to the temptation with as little firmness, and accepts the price of his fellow creatures liberty with as little reluctance as the enlightened merchant.

Accordingly he falls on his neighbours, and a desperate battle ensues. If he prevails and takes prisoners, he gratifies his avarice by selling them; but, if his party be vanquished, and he falls into the hands of the enemy, he is put to death: for, as he has been known to foment their quarrels, it is thought dangerous to let him survive, and no ransom can save him, though all other prisoners may be redeemed. We have fire-arms, bows and arrows, broad two-edged swords and javelins: we have shields also which cover a man from head to foot. All are taught the use of these weapons; even our women are warriors, and march boldly out to fight along with the men. Our whole district is a kind of militia: on a certain signal given, such as the firing of a gun at night, they all rise in arms and rush upon their enemy. It is perhaps something remarkable, that when our people march to the field a red flag or banner is borne before them. I was once a witness to a battle in our common.

We had been all at work in it one day as usual, when our people were suddenly attacked. I climbed a tree at some distance, from which I beheld the fight. There were many women as well as men on both sides; among others my mother was there, and armed with a broad sword. After fighting for a considerable time with great fury, and after many had been killed our people obtained the victory, and took their enemy's Chief prisoner. He was carried off in great triumph, and, though he offered a large ransom for his life, he was put to death. A virgin of note among our enemies had been slain in the battle, and her arm was exposed in our market-place, where our trophies were always exhibited. The spoils were divided according to the merit of the warriors. Those prisoners which were not sold or redeemed we kept as slaves: but how different was their condition from that of the slaves in the West Indies! With us they do no more work than other members of the community, even their masters; their food, clothing and lodging were nearly the same as theirs, (except that they were not permitted to eat with those who were free-born); and there was scarce any other difference between them, than a superior degree of importance which the head of a family possesses in our state, and that authority which, as such, he exercises over every part of his household. Some of these slaves have even slaves under them as their own property, and for their own use.

As to religion, the natives believe that there is one Creator of all things, and that he lives in the sun, and is girted round with a belt that he may never eat or drink; but, according to some, he smokes a pipe, which is our own favourite luxury. They believe he governs events, especially our deaths or captivity; but, as for the doctrine of eternity, I do not remember to have ever heard of it: some however believe in the transmigration of souls in a certain degree. Those spirits, which are not transmigrated, such as our dear friends or relations, they believe always attend them, and guard them from the bad spirits or their foes. For this reason they always before eating, as I have observed, put some small portion of the meat, and pour some of their drink, on the ground for them; and they often make oblations of the blood of beasts or fowls at their graves. I was very fond of my mother, and almost constantly with her. When she went to make these oblations at her mother's tomb, which was a kind of small solitary thatched house, I sometimes attended her. There she made her libations, and spent most of the night in cries and lamentations. I have been often extremely terrified on these occasions. The loneliness of the place, the darkness of the night, and the ceremony of libation, naturally awful and gloomy, were heightened by my mother's lamentations; and these, concuring with the cries of doleful birds, by which these places were frequented, gave an inexpressible terror to the scene.

We compute the year from the day on which the sun crosses the line, and on its setting that evening there is a general shout throughout the land; at least I can speak from my own knowledge throughout our vicinity. The people at the same time make a great noise with rattles, not unlike the basket rattles used by children here, though much larger, and hold up their hands to heaven for a blessing. It is then the greatest offerings are made; and those children whom our wise men foretel will be fortunate are then presented to different people. I remember many used to come to see me, and I was carried about to others for that purpose. They have many offerings, particularly at full moons; generally two at harvest before the fruits are taken out of the ground: and when any young animals are killed, sometimes they offer up part of them as a sacrifice. These offerings, when made by one of the heads of a family, serve for the whole. I remember we often had them at my father's and my uncle's, and their families have been present. Some of our offerings are eaten with bitter herbs. We had a saying among us to any one of a cross temper, 'That if they were to be eaten, they should be eaten with bitter herbs.'

We practised circumcision like the Jews, and made offerings and feasts on that occasion in the same manner as they did. Like them also, our children were named from some event, some circumstance, or fancied foreboding at the time of their birth. I was named *Olaudah*, which, in our language, signifies vicissitude or fortune also, one favoured, and having a loud voice and well spoken. I remember we never polluted the name of the object of our adoration; on the contrary, it was always mentioned with the greatest reverence; and we were totally unacquainted with swearing, and all those terms of abuse and reproach which find their way so readily and copiously into the languages of more civilized people. The only expressions of that kind I remember were 'May you rot, or may you swell, or may a beast take you.'

I have before remarked that the natives of this part of Africa are extremely cleanly. This necessary habit of decency was with us a part of religion, and therefore we had many purifications and washings; indeed almost as many, and used on the same occasions, if my recollection does not fail me, as the Jews. Those that touched the dead at any time were obliged to wash and purify themselves before they could enter a dwelling-house. Every woman too, at certain times, was forbidden to come into a dwelling-house, or touch any person, or any thing we ate. I was so fond of my mother I could not keep from her, or avoid touching her at some of those periods, in consequence of which I was obliged to be kept out with her, in a little house made for that purpose, till offering was made, and then we were purified.

Though we had no places of public worship, we had priests and magicians, or wise men. I do not remember whether they had different offices, or whether they were united in the same persons, but they were held in great reverence by the people. They calculated our time, and foretold events, as their name imported, for we called them Ah-affoe-way-cah, which signifies calculators or yearly men, our year being called Ah-affoe. They wore their beards, and when they died they were succeeded by their sons. Most of their implements and things of value were interred along with them. Pipes and tobacco were also put into the grave with the corpse, which was always perfumed and ornamented, and animals were offered in sacrifice to them. None accompanied their funerals but those of the same profession or tribe. These buried them after sunset, and always returned from the grave by a different way from that which they went.

These magicians were also our doctors or physicians. They practised bleeding by cupping; and were very successful in healing wounds and expelling poisons. They had likewise some extraordinary method of discovering jealousy, theft, and poisoning; the success of which no doubt they derived from their unbounded influence over the credulity and superstition of the people. I do not remember what those methods were, except that as to poisoning: I recollect an instance or two, which I hope it will not be deemed impertinent here to insert, as it may serve as a kind of specimen of the rest, and is still used by the negroes in the West Indies. A virgin had been poisoned, but it was not known by whom: the doctors ordered the corpse to be taken up by some persons, and carried to the grave. As soon as the bearers had raised it on their shoulders, they seemed seized with some[F] sudden impulse, and ran to and fro unable to stop themselves. At last, after having passed through a number of thorns and prickly bushes unhurt, the corpse fell from them close to a house, and defaced it in the fall; and, the owner being taken up, he immediately confessed the poisoning[G].

The natives are extremely cautious about poison. When they buy any eatable the seller kisses it all round before the buyer, to shew him it is not poisoned; and the same is done when any meat or drink is presented, particularly to a stranger. We have serpents of different kinds, some of which are esteemed ominous when they appear in our houses, and these we never molest. I remember two of those ominous snakes, each of which was as thick as the calf of a man's leg, and in colour resembling a dolphin in the water, crept at different times into my mother's night-house, where I always lay with her, and coiled themselves into folds, and each time they crowed like a cock. I was desired by some of our wise men to touch these, that I might be interested in the good omens, which I did, for they were quite harmless, and would tamely suffer themselves to be handled; and then they were put into a large open earthen pan, and set on one side of the highway. Some of our snakes, however, were poisonous: one of them crossed the road one day when I was standing on it, and passed between my feet without offering to touch me, to the great surprise of many who saw it; and these incidents were accounted by the wise men, and therefore by my mother and the rest of the people, as remarkable omens in my favour.

Such is the imperfect sketch my memory has furnished me with of the manners and customs of a people among whom I first drew my breath. And here I cannot forbear suggesting what has long struck me very forcibly, namely, the strong analogy which even by this sketch, imperfect as it is, appears to prevail in the manners and customs of my countrymen and those of the Jews, before they reached the Land of Promise, and particularly the patriarchs while they were yet in that pastoral state which is described in Genesis—an analogy, which alone would induce me to think that the one people had sprung from the other. Indeed this is the opinion of Dr. Gill, who, in his commentary on Genesis, very ably deduces the pedigree of the Africans from Afer and Afra, the descendants of Abraham by Keturah his wife and concubine (for both these titles are applied to her). It is also conformable to the sentiments of Dr. John Clarke, formerly Dean of Sarum, in his Truth of the Christian Religion: both these authors concur in ascribing to us this original. The reasonings of these gentlemen are still further confirmed by the scripture chronology; and if any further corroboration were required, this resemblance in so many respects is a strong evidence in support of the opinion. Like the Israelites in their primitive state, our government was conducted by our chiefs or judges, our wise men and elders; and the head of a family with us enjoyed a similar authority over his household with that which is ascribed to Abraham and the other patriarchs. The law of retaliation obtained almost universally with us as with them: and even their religion appeared to have shed upon us a ray of its glory, though broken and spent in its passage, or eclipsed by the cloud with which time, tradition, and ignorance might have enveloped it; for we had our circumcision (a rule I believe peculiar to that people:) we had also our sacrifices and burnt-offerings, our washings and purifications, on the same occasions as they had.

As to the difference of colour between the Eboan Africans and the modern Jews, I shall not presume to account for it. It is a subject which has engaged the pens of men of both genius and learning, and is far above my strength. The most able and Reverend Mr. T. Clarkson, however, in his much admired Essay on the Slavery and Commerce of the Human Species, has ascertained the cause, in a manner that at once solves every objection on that account, and, on my mind at least, has produced the fullest conviction. I shall therefore refer to that performance for the theory[H], contenting myself with extracting a fact as related by Dr. Mitchel[I]. "The Spaniards, who have inhabited America, under the torrid zone, for any time, are become as dark coloured as our native Indians of Virginia; of which *I myself have been a witness.*" There is also another instance[J] of a Portuguese settlement at Mitomba, a river in Sierra Leona; where the inhabitants are bred from a mixture of the first Portuguese discoverers with the natives, and are now become in their complexion, and in the woolly quality of their hair, *perfect negroes*, retaining however a smattering of the Portuguese language.

These instances, and a great many more which might be adduced, while they shew how the complexions of the same persons vary in different climates, it is hoped may tend also to remove the prejudice that some conceive against the natives of Africa on account of their colour. Surely the minds of the Spaniards did not change with their complexions! Are there not causes enough to which the apparent inferiority of an African may be ascribed, without limiting the goodness of God, and supposing he forbore to stamp understanding on certainly his own image, because "carved in ebony." Might it not naturally be ascribed to their situation? When they come among Europeans, they are ignorant of their language, religion, manners, and customs. Are any pains taken to teach them these? Are they treated as men? Does not slavery itself depress the mind, and extinguish all its fire and every noble sentiment? But, above all, what advantages do not a refined people possess over those who are rude and uncultivated. Let the polished and haughty European recollect that his ancestors were once, like the Africans, uncivilized, and even barbarous. Did Nature make *them* inferior to their sons? and should *they too* have been made slaves? Every rational mind answers, No. Let such reflections as these melt the pride of their superiority into sympathy for the wants and miseries of their sable brethren, and compel them to acknowledge, that understanding is not confined to feature or colour. If, when they look round the world, they feel exultation, let it be tempered with benevolence to others, and gratitude to God, "who hath made of one blood all nations of men for to dwell on all the face of the earth[K]; and whose wisdom is not our wisdom, neither are our ways his ways."

FOOTNOTES:

[A]See Benezet's "Account of Guinea" throughout.

[B]When I was in Smyrna I have frequently seen the Greeks dance after this manner.

[C]The bowl is earthen, curiously figured, to which a long reed is fixed as a tube. This tube is sometimes so long as to be born by one, and frequently out of grandeur by two boys.

[D]When I was in Smyrna I saw the same kind of earth, and brought some of it with me to England; it resembles musk in strength, but is more delicious in scent, and is not unlike the smell of a rose.

[E]See Benezet's Account of Africa throughout.

[F]See also Leut. Matthew's Voyage, p. 123.

[G]An instance of this kind happened at Montserrat in the West Indies in the year 1763. I then belonged to the Charming Sally, Capt. Doran.—The chief mate, Mr. Mansfield, and some of the crew being one day on shore, were present at the burying of a poisoned negro girl. Though they had often heard of the circumstance of the running in such cases, and had even seen it, they imagined it to be a trick of the corpse-bearers. The mate therefore desired two of the sailors to take up the coffin, and carry it to the grave. The sailors, who were all of the same opinion, readily obeyed; but they had scarcely raised it to their shoulders, before they began to run furiously about, quite unable to direct themselves, till, at last, without intention, they came to the hut of him who had poisoned the girl. The coffin then immediately fell from their shoulders against the hut, and damaged part of the wall. The owner of the hut was taken into custody on this, and confessed the poisoning.—I give this story as it was related by the mate and crew on their return to the ship. The credit which is due to it I leave with the reader.

[H]Page 178 to 216.

[I]Philos. Trans. Nº 476, Sect. 4, cited by Mr. Clarkson, p. 205.

[J]Same page.

[K]Acts, c. xvii. v. 26

APPENDIX 3

REPARATION INTRODUCED IN CONGRESS

Introduced in 01/03/2019) House
116th CONGRESS
1st Session
H. R. 40 H. R. 40

To address the fundamental injustice, cruelty, brutality, and inhumanity of slavery in the United States and the 13 American colonies between 1619 and 1865 and to establish a commission to study and consider a national apology and proposal for reparations for the institution of slavery, its subsequent de jure and de facto racial and economic discrimination against African-Americans, and the impact of these forces on living African-Americans, to make recommendations to the Congress on appropriate remedies, and for other purposes.

IN THE HOUSE OF REPRESENTATIVES

January 3, 2019

Ms. Jackson Lee (for herself, Mr. Serrano, Mr. Cohen, Mr. Khanna, Mr. Meeks, Ms. Moore, Ms. Jayapal, Mr. Johnson of Georgia, Mr. Payne, Ms. Clarke of New York, Ms. Johnson of Texas, Mrs. Beatty, Ms. Schakowsky, Mr. Thompson of

Mississippi, Ms. Lee of California, Mr. Green of Texas, Ms. Norton, Mr. Rush, Mr. Nadler, Mr. Danny K. Davis of Illinois, Mr. Engel, Mr. Richmond, Ms. Bass, and Mr. Evans) introduced the following bill; which was referred to the Committee on the Judiciary

A BILL

To address the fundamental injustice, cruelty, brutality, and inhumanity of slavery in the United States and the 13 American colonies between 1619 and 1865 and to establish a commission to study and consider a national apology and proposal for reparations for the institution of slavery, its subsequent de jure and de facto racial and economic discrimination against African-Americans, and the impact of these forces on living African-Americans, to make recommendations to the Congress on appropriate remedies, and for other purposes.

Be it enacted by the Senate and House of Representatives of the United States of America in Congress assembled,

SECTION 1. Short title.

This Act may be cited as the "Commission to Study and Develop Reparation Proposals for African-Americans Act".

SEC. 2. Findings and purpose.

(a) Findings.—The Congress finds that—

(1) approximately 4,000,000 Africans and their descendants were enslaved in the United States and colonies that became the United States from 1619 to 1865;

(2) the institution of slavery was constitutionally and statutorily sanctioned by the Government of the United States from 1789 through 1865;

(3) the slavery that flourished in the United States constituted an immoral and inhumane deprivation of Africans' life, liberty, African citizenship rights, and cultural heritage, and denied them the fruits of their own labor;

(4) a preponderance of scholarly, legal, community evidentiary documentation and popular culture markers constitute the basis for inquiry into the on-going effects of the institution of slavery and its legacy of persistent systemic structures of discrimination on living African-Americans and society in the United States; and

(5) following the abolition of slavery the United States Government, at the Federal, State, and local level, continued to perpetuate, condone and often profit from practices that continued to brutalize and disadvantage African-Americans, including share cropping, convict leasing, Jim Crow, redlining, unequal education, and disproportionate treatment at the hands of the criminal justice system; and

(6) as a result of the historic and continued discrimination, African-Americans continue to suffer debilitating economic, educational, and health hardships including but not limited to having nearly 1,000,000 black people incarcerated; an unemployment rate more than twice the current white unemployment rate; and an average of less than ⅟16 of the wealth of white families, a disparity which has worsened, not improved over time.

(b) Purpose.—The purpose of this Act is to establish a commission to study and develop Reparation proposals for African-Americans as a result of—

(1) the institution of slavery, including both the Trans-Atlantic and the domestic "trade" which existed from 1565 in colonial Florida and from 1619 through 1865 within the other colonies that became the United States, and which included the Federal and State governments which constitutionally and statutorily supported the institution of slavery;

(2) the de jure and de facto discrimination against freed slaves and their descendants from the end of the Civil War to the present, including economic, political, educational, and social discrimination;

(3) the lingering negative effects of the institution of slavery and the discrimination described in paragraphs (1) and (2) on living African-Americans and on society in the United States;

(4) the manner in which textual and digital instructional resources and technologies are being used to deny the inhumanity of slavery and the crime against humanity of people of African descent in the United States;

(5) the role of Northern complicity in the Southern based institution of slavery;

(6) the direct benefits to societal institutions, public and private, including higher education, corporations, religious and associational;

(7) and thus, recommend appropriate ways to educate the American public of the Commission's findings;

(8) and thus, recommend appropriate remedies in consideration of the Commission's findings on the matters described in paragraphs (1), (2), (3), (4), (5), and (6); and

(9) submit to the Congress the results of such examination, together with such recommendations.

SEC. 3. Establishment and duties.

(a) Establishment.—There is established the Commission to Study and Develop Reparation Proposals for African-Americans (hereinafter in this Act referred to as the "Commission").

(b) Duties.—The Commission shall perform the following duties:

(1) Identify, compile and synthesize the relevant corpus of evidentiary documentation of the institution of slavery which existed within the United States and the colonies that became the United States from 1619 through 1865. The Commission's documentation and examination shall include but not be limited to the facts related to—

(A) the capture and procurement of Africans;

(B) the transport of Africans to the United States and the colonies that became the United States for the purpose of enslavement, including their treatment during transport;

(C) the sale and acquisition of Africans as chattel property in interstate and intrastate commerce;

(D) the treatment of African slaves in the colonies and the United States, including the deprivation of their freedom, exploitation of their labor, and destruction of their culture, language, religion, and families; and

(E) the extensive denial of humanity, sexual abuse and the chatellization of persons.

(2) The role which the Federal and State governments of the United States supported the institution of slavery in constitutional and statutory provisions, including the extent to which such governments prevented, opposed, or restricted efforts of formerly enslaved Africans and their descendants to repatriate to their homeland.

(3) The Federal and State laws that discriminated against formerly enslaved Africans and their descendants who were deemed United States citizens from 1868 to the present.

(4) The other forms of discrimination in the public and private sectors against freed African slaves and their descendants who were deemed United States citizens from 1868 to the present, including redlining, educational funding discrepancies, and predatory financial practices.

(5) The lingering negative effects of the institution of slavery and the matters described in paragraphs (1), (2), (3), (4), (5), and (6) on living African-Americans and on society in the United States.

(6) Recommend appropriate ways to educate the American public of the Commission's findings.

(7) Recommend appropriate remedies in consideration of the Commission's findings on the matters described in paragraphs (1), (2), (3), (4), (5), and (6). In making such recommendations, the Commission shall address among other issues, the following questions:

(A) How such recommendations comport with international standards of remedy for wrongs and injuries caused by the State, that include full reparations and special measures, as understood by various relevant international protocols, laws, and findings.

(B) How the Government of the United States will offer a formal apology on behalf of the people of the United States for the perpetration of gross human rights violations and crimes against humanity on African slaves and their descendants.

(C) How Federal laws and policies that continue to disproportionately and negatively affect African-Americans as a group, and those that perpetuate the lingering effects, materially and psycho-social, can be eliminated.

(D) How the injuries resulting from matters described in paragraphs (1), (2), (3), (4), (5), and (6) can be reversed and provide appropriate policies, programs, projects and recommendations for the purpose of reversing the injuries.

(E) How, in consideration of the Commission's findings, any form of compensation to the descendants of enslaved African is calculated.

(F) What form of compensation should be awarded, through what instrumentalities and who should be eligible for such compensation.

(G) How, in consideration of the Commission's findings, any other forms of rehabilitation or restitution to African descendants is warranted and what the form and scope of those measures should take.

(c) Report to congress.—The Commission shall submit a written report of its findings and recommendations to the Congress not later than the date which is one year after the date of the first meeting of the Commission held pursuant to section 4(c).

SEC. 4. Membership.

(a) Number and appointment.— (1) The Commission shall be composed of 13 members, who shall be appointed, within 90 days after the date of enactment of this Act, as follows:

(A) Three members shall be appointed by the President.

(B) Three members shall be appointed by the Speaker of the House of Representatives.

(C) One member shall be appointed by the President pro tempore of the Senate.

(D) Six members shall be selected from the major civil society and reparations organizations that have historically championed the cause of reparatory justice.

(2) All members of the Commission shall be persons who are especially qualified to serve on the Commission by virtue of their education, training, activism or experience, particularly in the field of African-American studies and reparatory justice.

(b) Terms.—The term of office for members shall be for the life of the Commission. A vacancy in the Commission shall not affect the powers of the Commission and shall be filled in the same manner in which the original appointment was made.

(c) First meeting.—The President shall call the first meeting of the Commission within 120 days after the date of the enactment of this Act or within 30 days after the date on which legislation is enacted making appropriations to carry out this Act, whichever date is later.

(d) Quorum.—Seven members of the Commission shall constitute a quorum, but a lesser number may hold hearings.

(e) Chair and vice chair.—The Commission shall elect a Chair and Vice Chair from among its members. The term of office of each shall be for the life of the Commission.

(f) Compensation.— (1) Except as provided in paragraph (2), each member of the Commission shall receive compensation at the daily equivalent of the annual rate of basic pay payable for GS–18 of the General Schedule under section 5332 of title 5, United States Code, for each day, including travel time, during which he or she is engaged in the actual performance of duties vested in the Commission.

(2) A member of the Commission who is a full-time officer or employee of the United States or a Member of Congress shall receive no additional pay, allowances, or benefits by reason of his or her service to the Commission.

(3) All members of the Commission shall be reimbursed for travel, subsistence, and other necessary expenses incurred by

them in the performance of their duties to the extent authorized by chapter 57 of title 5, United States Code.

SEC. 5. Powers of the Commission.

(a) Hearings and sessions.—The Commission may, for the purpose of carrying out the provisions of this Act, hold such hearings and sit and act at such times and at such places in the United States, and request the attendance and testimony of such witnesses and the production of such books, records, correspondence, memoranda, papers, and documents, as the Commission considers appropriate. The Commission may invoke the aid of an appropriate United States district court to require, by subpoena or otherwise, such attendance, testimony, or production.

(b) Powers of subcommittees and members.—Any subcommittee or member of the Commission may, if authorized by the Commission, take any action which the Commission is authorized to take by this section.

(c) Obtaining official data.—The Commission may acquire directly from the head of any department, agency, or instrumentality of the executive branch of the Government, available information which the Commission considers useful in the discharge of its duties. All departments, agencies, and instrumentalities of the executive branch of the Government shall cooperate with the Commission with respect to such information and shall furnish all information requested by the Commission to the extent permitted by law.

SEC. 6. Administrative provisions.

(a) Staff.—The Commission may, without regard to section 5311(b) of title 5, United States Code, appoint and fix the compensation of such personnel as the Commission considers appropriate.

(b) Applicability of certain civil service laws.—The staff of the Commission may be appointed without regard to the provisions of title 5, United States Code, governing appointments in the competitive service, and without regard to the provisions of chapter 51 and subchapter III of chapter 53 of such title relating to classification and General Schedule pay rates, except that the compensation of any employee of the Commission may not exceed a rate equal to the annual rate of basic pay payable for GS–18 of the General Schedule under section 5332 of title 5, United States Code.

(c) Experts and consultants.—The Commission may procure the services of experts and consultants in accordance with the provisions of section 3109(b) of title 5, United States Code, but at rates for individuals not to exceed the daily equivalent of the highest rate payable under section 5332 of such title.

(d) Administrative support services.—The Commission may enter into agreements with the Administrator of General Services for procurement of financial and administrative services necessary for the discharge of the duties of the Commission. Payment for such services shall be made by reimbursement from funds of the Commission in such amounts as may be agreed upon by the Chairman of the Commission and the Administrator.

(e) Contracts.—The Commission may—

(1) procure supplies, services, and property by contract in accordance with applicable laws and regulations and to the extent or in such amounts as are provided in appropriations Acts; and

(2) enter into contracts with departments, agencies, and instrumentalities of the Federal Government, State agencies, and private firms, institutions, and agencies, for the conduct of research or surveys, the preparation of reports, and other activities necessary for the discharge of the duties of the Commission, to the extent or in such amounts as are provided in appropriations Acts.

SEC. 7. Termination.

The Commission shall terminate 90 days after the date on which the Commission submits its report to the Congress under section 3(c).

SEC. 8. Authorization of appropriations.

To carry out the provisions of this Act, there are authorized to be appropriated $12,000,000.

APPENDIX 4

In the last ten years, a worldwide movement has emerged for reparations to various previously subordinated groups for past wrongs. This paper discusses the movement for reparations to the continent of Africa. It begins with a discussion of the United Nations-sponsored World Conference against Racism, Racial Discrimination, Xenophobia and Related Intolerance held in Durban, South Africa, in September 2001. It then traces the discussion of reparations to Africa back to the Group of Eminent Persons (GEP) established in the early 1990s by the Organization of African Unity to pursue reparations for slavery and (perhaps) other wrongs perpetrated on Africa. Only three members of this group are still active: they are J. F. Ade Ajayi, Ali A. Mazrui, and Dudley Thompson. The present author interviewed all three in December 2002. An essay by J. F. Ade Ajayi is included in this volume.

THE DURBAN CONFERENCE AGAINST RACISM

At the Durban Conference against Racism, it was suggested that the Western world owed reparations to Africa. These reparations would be for the slave trade and colonialism, and even for the post-colonial era. The Declaration issued as the Final Document of the Conference stated: "We acknowledge that slavery and the slave trade... are a crime against humanity, and should always have been so, especially the trans-Atlantic slave trade, and are among the major sources and manifestations of racism, racial discrimination, xenophobia and related intolerance... We recognize that colonialism has led to racism, racial discrimination, xenophobia and related intolerance." Moreover, the Declaration stated that victims of violations of their human rights as a result of racism and related wrongs should have "the right to seek just and adequate reparation or satisfaction."

Several African countries supported this claim. For example, Ali Mohamed Osman Yassin, Minister of Justice of Sudan, made a statement explicitly linking the slave trade to the current problems of Africa:

"The slave trade, particularly against Africans, was an appalling tragedy in its abhorrent barbarism, enormous magnitude, institutionalized nature, transnational dimension and particularly in its negation of the essence of the victims. Africa's economic marginalization started with the deprivation of its manpower by the slave trade, followed by uneven exploitation and the siphoning of its natural resources during the colonial era. It is culminating today in economic globalization, where Africa lacks the capacity to compete commercially in the world economy" (United Nations 2001: 8).

Similarly, Enoch Kavindele, Vice-President of Zambia, demanded reparations:

"We have come to Durban to liberate ourselves from the historical injustices of slavery and servitude and now want to emphasize that slavery should be remembered not only as an appalling tragedy, but also as a factor which for centuries deprived Africa of her human and natural resources. Africa requests an audience, so the world can take responsibility for the crimes of slavery and colonialism... [T]he slave trade was the greatest practical evil which has ever afflicted the human race. And though we agree that many other peoples and races have been victims of discrimination and intolerance, the cry on the continent is that while every one of those groups have [sic] been adequately redressed for wrongs committed in the past, Africans continue to suffer" (United Nations 2001: 4).

Both these statements reflected the official viewpoint put forward prior to the Durban Conference by the African Regional Preparatory Conference for the World Conference. This Preparatory Conference affirmed that "[the] slave trade is a unique tragedy in the history of humanity, particularly against Africans–a crime against humanity which is unparalleled". It made an explicit connection between the slave trade and Africa's current problems, noting "the consequence of this tragedy [the slave trade] accentuated by those of colonialism and apartheid have resulted in substantial and lasting economic, political and cultural damage to African peoples and are still present in the form of damage caused to the descendants of the victims, the perpetuation of the prejudice against Africans in the Continent, and people of African descent in the Diaspora". The Conference also noted that "other groups which were subject to other scourges and injustices have received repeated apologies from different countries as well as ample reparations."

Not all African leaders supported this viewpoint, however. Just prior to the Durban Conference, the President of Senegal, Abdoulaye Wade, said that if reparations were to be paid for slavery, then he himself might be liable to pay them, as his ancestors had owned thousands of slaves. He found the proposal for monetary compensation for slavery insulting: "It is absurd... that you could pay up a certain number of dollars and then slavery ceases to exist, is cancelled out and there is the receipt to prove it" (Ba 2001). At the African preparatory Conference, he also angered participants by arguing that there was far more racism and xenophobic violence within Africa than against Africans in Europe (McGreal 2001).

Wade's minority view suggests that under the populist and rhetorical appeal of a call for reparations to Africa may lie an unwillingness to deal with far more complex issues of the real causes of that continent's severe underdevelopment. Promotion of a bitter call for reparations is an easy way to deflect attention from internal African politics, and the many abuses of human rights by African dictators. The Nigerian Nobel-prize winning writer Wole Soyinka, for example, pointed out that M. K. O. Abiola, the founder of the reparations movement (see below), had himself become a prisoner of the then dictator of Nigeria, Sani Abacha. "Abiola… is today himself enslaved by one of the new breed of slave dealers, who actually boasts of power over the most heavily populated, most talented slave market that the African world has ever known. This mockery of history is complete even down to the underground railroad on which hundreds travel every day, this author [Soyinka] included" (Soyinka 1999: 73). Moreover, Soyinka argued, reparations began at home: "[R]eparations, like charity, should begin at home, and the wealth of the Mobutus, the Babangidas, the Abachas … should be utilized as down payment" (*ibid.:* 86).

The focus only on Africa's relations with the West, but not on its relations with other regions, also raises some uncomfortable issues. Not only the Western world, but also the Arab world, looked to Africa for slaves. For both Ali Mazrui and J. F. Ade Ajayi, the discomfort of focusing only on the West is easily solved. Mazrui believes that the Arab slave trade was qualitatively different from the Atlantic trade. The Western slavers were the most race-conscious, asserts Mazrui, whereas "Islam went further than others to encourage *emancipation* of slaves", and also had several other customs which made it possible to integrate slaves into free society, for example by recognized alliances between free males and slave women (Mazrui 2002: 41, emphasis in original). Ajayi (2002: 8) also argues that the trans-Atlantic slave trade "bred racism that was never a part of the Muslim Arab world as Arabs enslaved both whites and blacks, preached the virtue of manumission, and opened the possibility for some fortunate black slaves to rise to high positions as scholars, or diplomats or successful generals".

Other commentators are not so forgiving of Arab slavers. Wole Soyinka (1999: 53-55) sees no difference between the two: "Islam… inaugurated the era of slave raids on the black continent for Arab slave markets… Even today, you will encounter ghettoes in many Arab countries peopled entirely by descendants of those slaves… [T]he Africa, on behalf of whom reparations are sought, is that Africa that was enslaved under the divine authority of the islamic and christian gods, their earthly plenipotentiaries, and commercial stormtroopers… It simply seems to me rather presumptuous to offer absolution to the practitioner of a dehumanizing trade through an exercise in comparative degrees of abuse."

Yet some thoughtful, scholarly Africans nevertheless argue for reparations from the West, on legal, moral and material grounds. Given the current worldwide interest in apologies and compensation for myriad past wrongs, it is unlikely that the rhetoric of the Durban Conference will disappear.

The Group of Eminent Persons

The movement for reparations originated in the Organization of African Unity (OAU), now succeeded by the African Union (AU). At a meeting in Abuja, Nigeria on 28 June 1992, the OAU swore in a 12-member Group of Eminent Persons. The Group's mandate was to pursue the goal of reparations to Africa. The original Chair of the Group was the wealthy Nigerian businessman, Chief Bashorun M. K. O. Abiola, who was later elected President of Nigeria, although never permitted to take office. Other members were the Nigerian historian J. F. Ade Ajayi; Professor Samir Amin of Egypt; US Congressman R. Dellums; Professor Josef Ki-Zerbo of Burkina Faso; Mme Gracha Machel, formerly First Lady of Mozambique, and a political activist in her own right (and later the wife of Nelson Mandela); Miriam Makeba, the South African singer; the Kenyan social scientist Ali Mazrui (based in the United States); Professor M. M'Bow, former Director-General of UNESCO; former President A. Pereira of Cape Verde; Ambassador Alex Quaison-Sackey, former foreign minister in the government of Kwame Nkrumah of Ghana; and the Jamaican lawyer and diplomat Dudley S. Thompson[4]. It is not clear whether all 12 individuals were present at Abuja, or indeed if all were aware of their new role. As of December 2002, three members of the group were still actively pursuing reparations, mainly through their writings and via lectures at academic conferences and institutions. They were J. F. Ajayi, Ali Mazrui, and Dudley Thompson. According to Thompson, they still filed annual reports to the OAU/AU, although this author has not been able to locate any such reports[5]. According to Mazrui, there was very little contact among members of the Group, who acted in their individual capacities rather than as a collective[6].

The GEP was established at the suggestion of M. K. O. Abiola[7]. Abiola had apparently been influenced to take up this cause both by a chance discussion of the Holocaust with a Jewish businessman, and by his contacts with the Congressional Black Caucus in the United States[8]. In a speech delivered in London in 1992, Abiola said: "Our demand for reparations is based on the tripod of moral, historic, and legal arguments... Who knows what path Africa's social development would have taken if our great centres of civilization had not been razed in search of human cargo? Who knows how our economies would have developed...?" Abiola (1992: 910) went on to argue that international law applied (retroactively) to slavery, the slave trade and colonialism. "It is international law which compels Nigeria to pay her debts to western banks and financial institutions: it is international law which must now demand that the western nations pay us what they have owed us for six centuries."

The then-President of Nigeria, Ibrahim Babangida, promoted the idea of reparations and officially dedicated US$500,000 to it (although the Group apparently received these funds from Abiola's private purse, not from the Government of Nigeria)[9]. Babangida had discussed the idea of reparations as early as 1991 with the then presidents of Senegal and Togo, the three agreeing that the African debt "should be written off as part of the reparations due for 500 years of slavery of Africans in Western Europe and America"[10].

From 27 to 29 April 1993, the first (and, as far as this author can ascertain, last) "Pan-African Conference on Reparations" was held in Abuja, Nigeria, sponsored by the GEP and the Commission for Reparations of the Organization of African Unity (Mazrui 2002: 135). An official Proclamation was issued at this Conference. This Proclamation referred to the "moral debt" and "the debt of compensation" owed to Africa by countries that engaged in slavery and colonialism, and neo-colonialism[11]. It also called for the return of "stolen goods, artefacts, and other traditional treasures" (such as the campaign by the African Reparations Movement in Britain to have the Benin bronzes presently housed in the British Museum returned to Africa) (Soni n.d.). Compensation was envisaged in the form of "capital transfer and debt cancellation", as well as in a re-ordering of international relations to give Africa more representation in the "highest decision-making bodies" and, in particular, a permanent seat on the United Nations' Security Council12.

Six years later, in 1999, a "Truth Commission Conference" was held in Accra, Ghana. This Commission was apparently comprised of private individuals from nine African countries, the United States, the United Kingdom and three Caribbean countries (Mazrui 2002: 139). It concluded that "the root causes of Africa's problems today are the enslavement and colonization of African people over a 400-year period", that Africans were owed US$777 trillion in compensation (plus annual interest) and that, presumably in consequence of non-payment, there was no African debt to outsiders13. The final Declaration of the Truth Commission Conference does not give any indication of how it came up with the figure of US$777 trillion, in any case an absurd figure, given that the United States' Gross Domestic Product in 2001 was estimated at "only" US$10.082 trillion (CIA 2002).

The figure of US$777 trillion is decidedly larger than that proposed by an academic author on reparations, Daniel Tetteh Osabu-Kle. Nevertheless, the figure proposed by Osabu-Kle is also absurd. He believes that Africa is owed US$100 trillion in compensation. Osabu-Kle bases his estimate on the population difference between Africa and Asia, and on the assumption that without the slave trade and the alleged subsequent population decline in the continent, Africa would now be as heavily populated as Asia. He then assigns a value of US$75,000 to each "lost" person (on the basis of the Warsaw Convention for assigning value to loss of human life in aircraft crashes) reaching US$75 trillion for lost Africans, and adds a third of that total for compensation to diaspora Africans (Osabu-Kle 2000: 344-345). The members of the GEP themselves, however, do not assign a value to the reparations they seek. As Thompson argued, "[O]nce you begin to do that you... trivialize reparations and what it stands [for]... It is impossible to put a figure to killing millions of people, our ancestors"14.

As did Osabu-Kle, the GEP defined "Africa" broadly, to include both people living in Africa and members of the African diaspora; that is to say, descendants of Africans who lived outside of Africa. As Mazrui (2002: 60) put it, "We define *Global Africa* as the continent of Africa *plus* the Diaspora of enslavement (descendants of survivors of the Middle Passage) and the Diaspora of colonialism (the dispersal of Africans which continues to occur as a result of colonization and its aftermath)." This was also the view of the British jurist, Lord Anthony Gifford (1993: 10), who spoke at the 1993 conference on reparations in Abuja. "[A]ll Africans, on the continent of Africa and in the Diaspora, who suffer the consequences of the crime of mass kidnap and enslavement, have an interest in this claim... All Africans around the world have been affected in some way by the crime of slavery. Even those who have succeeded in a business or a profession have had to face racial prejudice at the least."

The idea of a global Africa draws upon the earlier Pan-Africanist tradition, started by the Caribbean-American Marcus Garvey in the 1920s. For Garvey, slavery was a collective trauma, which influenced all succeeding generations of Africans and people of African descent. "Slavery... was more than theft and the loss of freedom in forced labor, it deprived a people of their dreams and stripped them of their civilization" (Eyerman 2001: 91). The Pan-Africanist movement was revitalized in the early post-colonial period by such populist African leaders as Kwame Nkrumah. Dudley Thompson, who was in his mid-1980s when interviewed in December 2002, had long been involved in the Pan-Africanist movement, starting from his days as President of the West Indian Students' Association in Britain in the 1940s. Thompson knew Nkrumah15, and used Nkrumah's phrase, "We can no longer afford the luxury of delay", as evidence of his argument for reparations (Thompson 1999). In Thompson's view, there was a "primordial debt" owed to Africa16.

Precedents

There are two major precedents for reparations to Africa. They are reparations to Jews for the Holocaust, and the movement in the United States for reparations to African-Americans.

The issue of reparations to Jews for the Holocaust resurfaced in international discussion in the 1990s when Jewish groups began to demand that unpaid life insurance policies on victims of the Holocaust be paid, and that monies deposited by Jews in Swiss banks before and during the Second World War be paid to survivors of murdered Jews (Barkan 2000: 3-29, 88-111; Brooks 1999: 13-81). Increasingly, African-Americans and Africans became aware that "some" people—most especially Jews—seemed to be entitled to reparations for their suffering, while others were not. That in the view of many people in the formerly colonized world, Jews had become colonial oppressors of Palestinians merely compounded the problem. In some African eyes, it appeared that "white" victims of mass atrocities were entitled to compensation, while non-white victims were not. Thus Mazrui (2002: 87) asked: "How do twelve years of Jewish hell... compare to several centuries of Black enslavement?" Abiola (1992: 910) shortened the period of Jewish suffering even further, referring to the "six-year holocaust perpetrated against Jews by Hitler". Joseph Ndiaye, curator in 1998 of the Maison des Esclaves (House of Slaves) on the Island of Goree off Senegal, from which slaves apparently used to be shipped to the Americas, offered a similar opinion. He said: "We never stop hearing about the Holocaust, but how often do we dwell on the tragedy that took place here over 350 years; a tragedy that consumed tens of millions of lives?"17.

These statements reveal an understandable lack of knowledge of the situation of Jews in Europe. If one were to bring together their entire history of expulsions, mass murders and discrimination, one could argue that the Jews, like Africans, suffered for centuries, if not millennia, not for only six or twelve years. But the historical "truth" of the situation of European Jews is unlikely to affect such opinions as are expressed above. More important is the sense that white Jews take up an inordinate amount of the Western world's attention and sympathy, while black African suffering is ignored. Thus Jakaya Kikwete, Minister of Foreign Affairs of the United Republic of Tanzania, speaking at the Durban Conference, angrily made an explicit comparison of attention to the Holocaust, and neglect, as he saw it, of Africa's situation. "The Jews are being compensated for crimes committed against them during the Holocaust. There are many such examples. We do not understand why there is total hostility to the idea of reparation and compensation to Africa. What is it that is so blasphemous about it? Is it because Africa does not deserve it?... Africans deserve this. It is a matter of principle" (United Nations 2001: 5).

The GEP also drew upon the growing movement for reparations to African-Americans. A popular spokesperson calling for reparations to African-Americans was the eminent activist, Randall Robinson. Like Ali Mazrui, he too referred to the Jewish example. "As Germany and other interests that profited *owe* reparations to Jews following the holocaust of Nazi persecution, America and other interests that profited *owe* reparations to blacks following the holocaust of African slavery" (Robinson 2000: 9, emphasis in original). Therefore, said Robinson, "white society... must own up to slavery and acknowledge its debt to slavery's contemporary victims. It must, at long last, pay that debt in massive restitutions made to America's only involuntary members" (*ibid.:* 107). Further, Robinson believed strongly that Europe and America owed reparations to the continent of Africa. Again, he drew upon the Jewish example to make his point. "For twelve years Nazi Germany inflicted horrors upon European Jews. And Germany paid. It paid Jews individually. It paid the state of Israel. For two and a half centuries, Europe and America inflicted unimaginable horrors upon Africa and its people. Europe not only paid nothing to Africa in compensation, but followed the slave trade with the remapping of Africa for further economic exploitation" (*ibid.:* 204).

Within the United States, the demand for reparations takes several forms. One is a demand for an apology to African-Americans, as represented by a Bill unsuccessfully introduced into the US House of Representatives by a white Congressman, Tony Hall, in 1997[18]. Another is the movement to bring class-action civil lawsuits against corporations that have allegedly profited from the enslavement of African-Americans, such as the suit against Aetna Insurance, which in the 1990s apologized to blacks for underwriting insurance policies on slaves before 1863 (Hitt 2000: 41; Mazrui 2002: 8-9). Finally, there is the claim that the United States of America, as a country, owes some remedy to its African-American citizens. This is the claim made by Representative John Conyers, sponsor of H. R. 40, a Bill to establish a "Commission to Study Reparation Proposals for African-Americans", introduced in the House of Representatives on 6 January 1999[19]. In the early twenty-first century the most active group in the United States seeking reparations was N'COBRA, The National Coalition of Blacks for Reparations in America.

Aside from these two larger precedents, activists for reparations were aware of many other historic cases. Abiola, for example, cited reparations paid by Germany to its former enemies after the First World War, United States' reparations to Japanese-Americans interned during the Second World War, and American, Canadian and Australian reparations to indigenous peoples. He also noted reparations demanded of Iraq after the 1991 Gulf War (Abiola 1992: 910). Thompson added to these Poland's demands on Germany for compensation to Polish slave-labourers. Thompson also noted the irony that when slaves were freed in the British empire, compensation was paid not to the ex-slaves, but to their ex-owners, as compensation for lost property (a fact also alluded to by Ajayi, in his contribution to this volume). All of these cases, according to Thompson, were precedents for a legal claim of unjust enrichment (Thompson 1999: 2-3).

There are also quite recent precedents for reparations to Africa. There is a great deal of international interest in various forms of truth-telling, forgiveness, and possibilities for reconciliation, stemming from the innovative Truth and Reconciliation Commission (TRC) in post-apartheid South Africa. Ajayi cites the TRC in his essay in this volume. He also cites a French law of 2001 that recognizes the trans-Atlantic slave trade as a crime against humanity, and the admission by the Belgians in 2002 of their role in the murder of Patrice Lumumba, first President of independent Congo. All of these cases reflect a growing international social movement to recognize historic injustices.

The Wider Social Movement

The GEP used the term "reparations" to mean financial compensation. In international law, reparations include a variety of activities meant to repair or "make whole" relations between two groups, one of whom has victimized the other, including symbolic reparations such as apologies[20]. This more encompassing meaning of reparations was of little interest to the GEP: without financial compensation, all other forms of reparation were meaningless. As suggested above, the final form of financial compensation was not yet decided by the GEP. While cancellation of all of Africa's foreign debt (apparently to both governmental and private creditors) was advocated by NGOs at the Durban Conference, both Mazrui and Thompson felt that this was not a necessary claim, as the debt was unlikely to be paid in any case. The members of the GEP did advocate capital transfer in the form of a Marshall Plan for Africa, harkening back to the Marshall Plan that assisted Europe after the Second World War. Mazrui (2002: 67) referred to such a plan as the Middle Passage Plan, after the notorious Middle Passage voyage across the Atlantic endured by all Africans brought to the Americas as slaves.

Nor was the GEP interested in the finer points of legality of compensation. In his case for reparations, Abiola (1992: 910) claimed that there was a principle that "a state is liable for any injury suffered by another or by the other's nationals, such injury arising from the breach of any international obligations or from the breach of any principle of international customary law". But this is an anachronistic attribution of contemporary international law–and the contemporary world structure of states–to a period when neither existed. Slavery and the slave trade were not actually abolished in law until the late nineteenth and early twentieth centuries (Robertson 1999: 209). As Max Du Plessis (2003: 636, emphasis in original) notes, it is very difficult in law to argue that "the acts of slavery committed *then* amount to a violation of fundamental norms of international law *now*". It is even more difficult to argue that the law requires reparation for colonialism, which was legal under international law until 1945 at earliest (*ibid.:* 657). In the light of the weakness of legal claims for reparations, the case will have to be made via international political and moral debate.

As of 2003, the members of the GEP had had little success in starting a widespread movement for reparations to Africa, beyond the level of rhetoric. Many African non-governmental organizations and African-American organizations, supported the idea of reparations to Africa in principle, and participated in the NGO discussions of this topic at Durban and before[21]. More than this, the international NGO Forum at the World Conference against Racism also supported the idea of reparations to Africa. "Slave-holder nations, colonizers and occupying countries have unjustly enriched themselves at the expense of those people that they enslaved and colonized and whose land they have occupied. As these nations largely owe their political, economic and social domination to the exploitation of Africa, Africans and Africans in the Diaspora they should recognize their obligation to provide these victims just and equitable reparations"[22].

Nevertheless, by 2003 there were few groups actively dedicated to this issue. A group in Britain called the African Reparations Movement (ARM) had been very active on the Net, but was less active in 2003 as a consequence of the death of a financial benefactor who apparently had supported its website, which disappeared. There were small groups demanding reparations in Ghana and Kenya (Mazrui 2002). A "Jamaican Reparations Movement", naming Dudley Thompson as its Patron and connected to the Rastafarian religious movement, issued statements at the time of the Durban conference and beyond, but this author could not find any further evidence of its existence (JRM 2003). Up to 2002, and presumably beyond, the three active members of the GEP gave lectures, especially at universities, and tried to encourage students to form their own branches, for example, in Brazil[23].

One difficulty in starting an international movement for reparations to Africa is the problem of how to frame the question. The three active members of the GEP referred frequently to the work of Walter Rodney (1972)[24], a very influential member of the "underdevelopment" school of thought of the 1960s and 1970s. This school of thought, started by Andre Gunder Frank in 1967, argued that the lower level of development of the then "Third World" regions of the world was not a natural state, but a consequence of the *process* of underdevelopment caused by exploitative relations with the Western colonizers (Frank 1967). As Rodney (1972: 149) put it, "what was a slight difference [in levels of development] when the Portuguese sailed to West Africa in 1444 was a huge gap by the time that European robber statesmen sat down in Berlin 440 years later to decide who should steal which parts of Africa".

The idea that African underdevelopment was and is caused by its relations with the West has powerful rhetorical appeal. So does the idea that Western development, conversely, was a result of African exploitation and underdevelopment. The early work of Eric Williams (1966), a Caribbean historian, arguing that the slavery was the basis of Britain's wealth, still has resonance among contemporary commentators (Edmonson 2001).

These ideas provide a relatively simple–although, in this author's opinion, also partially correct (Howard 1978)–explanation for the tragic economic and political state of much of Africa today. For example, Osabu-Kle (2000: 333, 340) argued that "super profits from the labor of African slaves made possible the investments that resulted in the industrial revolution... African resources made the West rich and great! If Europeans were [sic] not greedy, Africa would have had the peace to develop on its own without being underdeveloped by anyone". Mazrui (1999: 1) also argued that "Africa Developed the West". "[T] he labor of Africa's sons and daughters was what the West needed for its industrial take-off", he believed, referring also to the "extractive imperative" as Africa's agricultural and mineral wealth were removed for Western use. In Thompson's view, "The debt is to do with the adjustment of the racial... situation... [T]he highly industrialized nations of the West... interrupted normal historical development, indigenous development by the Africans, and particularly West Africa. They interrupted it by the heinous crime of slavery. With over four centuries they abducted the strongest and the best and some of the youngest life blood for coming generations... They debilitated Africa"[25].

But even if one agrees with Rodney's controversial approach, there is a very long causal chain between slavery, colonialism and the current situation of Africans. Margaret Keck and Kathryn Sikkink (1998) explain that social movements for human rights are most likely to be successful when there is a short and recognizable connection between cause and effect. The evidence and logic needed to show how the slave trade caused underdevelopment in Africa today is detailed and complex. This is especially so because the slave trade was abolished by the British in 1807 and by the United States in 1808. Moreover, argue Keck and Sikkink (*ibid.:* 195), social movements are successful when direct harm can be demonstrated. While in retrospect, the direct harms of slavery endured by those enslaved are easy to identify, the direct harm visited upon their descendants is far less clear. It is, therefore, difficult to persuade those Western states (and their citizens) who might be expected to pay compensation that the often tragic situation of Africans and members of the African Diaspora alive today is a consequence in part of the actions of the West's own forebears.

The GEP also had some difficulty agreeing on an appropriate "frame" for the reparations claims. Without a clear frame, indicating precisely what is at issue, it is difficulty for any nascent social movement to attract allies to its cause (*ibid.:* 2 sq). The Group proposed, at minimum, reparations to Africa for the slave trade. However, there was disagreement among the Group's members as to whether reparations were also owed for colonialism or post-colonial relations. Mazrui felt that to extend the claim beyond slavery to colonialism would weaken the case for reparations: "It makes it difficult to win on both by mixing the two"[26]. Ajayi, by contrast, believed that reparations were also due for colonialism. As he argues in this volume, colonialism continued the worst characteristics of the slave trade. "Features of the slave trade and American slavery that characterized colonialism in Africa included racism, excessive violence and gross abuse of human rights. It was part of the propaganda of empire that Africans were lazy and had to be flogged to make them work... [R]acist colonialism... exploited, rather than developed, Africa" (Ajayi 2002: 3). Moreover, according to Ajayi, only Africans endured the double burden of both being enslaved and colonized, as compared to other parts of the world such as India27. Thompson saw a case for reparations not only for colonialism, but also for the post-colonial period. "Colonialism", he said, "is just a half step from slavery." As for the post-colonial period, "they gave us a crown but they kept the jewels". Moreover, in Thompson's view even the present era of globalization is characterized by international relations that require reparations. "Globalization is a crime... [U]s, I mean slaves and ex-slaves, we're far behind... and the technological age is moving us further and further away..."28. On balance, however, Thompson preferred to keep to the more restricted claim for reparations for slavery.

One must ask, therefore, what the future of a movement for reparations to Africa is likely to be, once the three still active members of the GEP are no longer able to continue their work for reparations. There does not seem to be any active group willing and able to take on their labours. The African Union, successor to the Organization of African States, does not appear to have taken up the idea of reparations as a focus of its activities. Moreover, as Thompson himself noted, reparations is not an issue that is of concern for most ordinary Africans, who are concerned with more mundane matters of day-to-day survival. "There's a vast majority, a large part... who feel that this is a matter of such a long time ago... that we should forget about it". The genesis and activities of the GEP may be remembered as a mere comment on Western-African relations, absent the organizational resources to enlarge upon their activities.

ABIOLA, M. K .O.
1992 "Why Reparations?", *West Africa*, 1-7 June: 910-911.

AJAYI, J. F. Ade
2002 "The Politics of Reparation in the Context of Globalisation", Distinguished Abiola Lecture, *African Studies Association*, Washington, D. C., 7 December 2002 (This paper is reprinted in French in this volume).

BA, D.
2001 "Senegal's Wade Calls Slave Reparations Absurd", *Independent Online*, published online on 11 August 2001, www.iol.co.za/general/news/newsprint.php? art_id=qw997554422285B252&sf=68.

BARKAN, E.
2000 *The Guilt of Nations: Restitution and Negotiating Historical Injustices* (New York: W. W. Norton).

BAZYLER, M. J.
2001 "The Holocaust Restitution Movement in Comparative Perspective", paper presented at the Association of Genocide Scholars, Fourth Biennial Conference, Minneapolis, MN.

BROOKS, R. L. (ed.)
1999 *When Sorry Isn't Enough: The Controversy over Apologies and Reparations for Human Injustice* (New York: New York University Press).

CIA (Central Intelligence Agency)
2002 *World Fact Book 2002*, Economy: United States, www.umsl.edu/services/govdocs/wofact2002/geos/us.html.

DU PLESSIS, M.
2003 "Historical Injustice and International Law: An Exploratory Discussion of Reparation for Slavery", *Human Rights Quarterly* 25 (3): 624-659.

EDMONDSON, L.
2001 "Reparations: Pan-African and Jewish Experiences", Symposium on Third World Views of the Holocaust, Northeastern University, Boston, April 18-20.

EYERMAN, R.
2001 *Cultural Trauma: Slavery and the Formation of African American Identity* (N.Y.: Cambridge University Press).

FRANK, A. G.
1967 *Capitalism and Underdevelopment in Latin America: Historical Studies of Chile and Brazil* (New York: Monthly Review Press).

GIFFORD, A. (Lord)
1993 "The legal basis of the claim for reparations", A paper presented to the First Pan-African Congress on Reparations, Abuja, Federal Republic of Nigeria, 27-29 April 1993, http://www.arm.arc.co.uk/legalBasis.html.

HITT, J. *et al.*
2000 "Making the Case for Racial Reparations", *Harper's Magazine*, 301 (1806): 37-51.

HOWARD, R.
1978 *Colonialism and Underdevelopment in Ghana* (London: Croom Helm).

JRM (Jamaica Reparations Movement)
2003 "Repairing the Damage, Redressing the Injustice", 28 February 2003, www.geocities.com/i_makeda/draftdocument.html.

KECK, M. E. & SIKKINK, K.

1998   *Activists Beyond Borders: Advocacy Networks in International Politics* (Ithaca, N.Y.: Cornell University Press).

MAZRUI, A. A.
1999   "From Slave Ship to Space Ship: Africa between Marginalization and Globalization", *African Studies Quarterly: the Online Journal for African Studies,* 2 (4), http://www.africa. ufl.edu/asq/v2/v2i4a2.htm.2002   *Black Reparations in the Era of Globalization* (Binghamton, N.Y.: Institute of Global Cultural Studies).

MAZRUI, A. A., LUTHULI, A. & WHITE, D.
2002   "The Campaign for Black Reparations: An African Initiative", Web site no longer accessible, hard copy available from author.

MCGREAL, C.
2001   "Turning Racism on its Head", *Mail and Guardian,* (Johannesburg) January 30, www.mg.co.za.

OSABU-KLE, D. T.
2000   "The African Reparation Cry: Rationale, Estimate, Prospects and Strategies", *Journal of Black Studies* 30 (3): 331-350.

ROBERTSON, G.
1999   *Crimes against Humanity: The Struggle for Global Justice* (New York: The New Press).

ROBINSON, R.
2000   *The Debt: What America Owes to Blacks* (New York: Dutton [Penguin]).

RODNEY, W.

1972 *How Europe Underdeveloped Africa* (London: Bogle-L'Ouverture Publications).

SONI, D.
n.d. "The British and the Benin Bronzes", ARM [African Reparations Movement] Information Sheet 4, www.arm.arc.co.uk/CRBBinfo4.html.

SOYINKA, W.
1999 *The Burden of Memory, the Muse of Forgiveness* (New York: Oxford University Press).

THOMPSON, D.
1999 "The Debt has Not Been Paid, the Accounts Have Not Been Settled", *African Studies Quarterly: the Online Journal for African Studies*, 2 (4), www.africa. ufl.edu/asq/v2/v2i4a4.htm.

UNITED NATIONS
2001 Press Release, "Acknowledgement of Past, Compensation Urged by Many Leaders in Continuing Debate at Racism Conference", RD/D/24, 2 September, www.unhchr.ch/huricane/huricane.nsf/view01.

WILLIAMS, E.
1966 [1944] *Capitalism and Slavery* (N.Y.: Capricorn Books).

ACKNOWLEDGEMENT

On May 14, 2000, Humphrey Amaechina gave me his last assignment on Earth. In his last letter, he asked me to write a good book titled "REPARATION TO AFRICA." It has taken me 20 years to complete Amaechina's homework.

I am indebted to so many people who have helped in making this dream a reality: Melody, for proofreading the manuscript and for isolating myself from the family for many years while working on this project. Jamike, my daughter for warning me not to change the title as I frequently did. Nathaniel Horowitz for his critical mind, stinging comments and editing.

I also thank my past and present students for their comments and for urging me to publish this work as soon as possible. Fakuade Michael Damilola and I spent many nights typing and proofreading the manuscript. I owe Dami tons of gratitude for his hard work.

Most importantly, I thank my friends and life partners – Pam Louis-Walden, Wayne, Sabato, Jason, Phoebe, Mike, Karen and Gene for their love and support. Pam and Chidi Obumneme bear witness to my visit to "exhume" Olauda, the adopted son of Ntsokara, Ezza - my ethnic homeland.

QUOTES

Olauda's story is more than a tale about bondage and justice, though slavery was an important part of his life. It is the story of one Igbo man who encountered this brutal world and learned how to survive in it, physically and spiritually. In telling the story of one who survived, Ikwueno tells the stories of countless others who did not. What is justice for Olauda and the muted voices?

Kamenu – is a universal law that holds all life together. The trans-Atlantic slave trade is sometimes considered as an ancestral karma and not a punishment from God. The human family has a complex and inseparable karma since we are, indeed, our own ancestors.

"In the first expressions of my grief I reproached my *fate* and wished I had never been born. I was ready to curse the tide that bore us, the gale that wafted my prison, and even the ship that conducted us; and I called on death to relieve me from the horrors I felt and dreaded, that I might be in that place." – Olauda Equiano

Institutional slavery in the African world (Africa, Caribbean, the Americas, and Europe) is an unfinished business. Africans, rightly or wrongly, believe that there is Karma at work in the cards life has dealt us.